The Coming of Globalization

Its Evolution and Contemporary Consequences

Richard Langhorne
Professor of Political Science
Director of the Center for Global Change and Governance
Rutgers University
USA

First published 2001 by
PALGRAVE
Houndmills, Basingstoke, Hampshire RG21 6XS and
175 Fifth Avenue, New York, N.Y. 10010
Companies and representatives throughout the world

PALGRAVE is the new global academic imprint of
St. Martin's Press LLC Scholarly and Reference Division and
Palgrave Publishers Ltd (formerly Macmillan Press Ltd).

ISBN 0–333–91777–4 hardback
ISBN 0–333–94718–5 paperback

This book is printed on paper suitable for recycling and
made from fully managed and sustained forest sources.

A catalogue record for this book is available
from the British Library.

Library of Congress Cataloging-in-Publication Data
Langhorne, Richard, 1940–
    The coming of globalization : its evolution and contemporary
    consequences / Richard Langhorne.
        p. cm.
    Includes bibliographical references and index.
    ISBN 0–333–91777–4 — ISBN 0–333–94718–5 (paper)
    1. Globalization. I. Title.

JZ1318 .L36 2000
303.4—dc21
                                            00–055688

10   9   8   7   6   5   4   3   2   1
10   09   08   07   06   05   04   03   02   01

Printed and bound in Great Britain by
Antony Rowe Ltd, Chippenham, Wiltshire

The Coming of Globalization

Also by Richard Langhorne

THE COLLAPSE OF THE CONCERT OF EUROPE: International Politics, 1890–1914

DIPLOMACY AND INTELLIGENCE DURING THE SECOND WORLD WAR (*editor*)

THE PRACTICE OF DIPLOMACY: Its Evolution, Theory and Administration (*with Keith Hamilton*)

For
Dr Norman Samuels, Provost,
and, through him, the Newark Campus of Rutgers University,
with respect and gratitude to colleagues and students alike

Contents

Acknowledgements

I am deeply grateful to the following for their help and encouragement. They need have no fear that any responsibility for what follows will be imputed to them: the responsibility is all mine. John Dunning, Yale and Kitty Ferguson, John Fousek, Edwin Hartman, David Hosford, Elizabeth Hull, Stephen Marshall and Alexander Motyl. Among them, I owe a very particular debt of gratitude to John Dunning for his help with the content of Chapter 2. It should also be said that this book would not have been written without the need to think about the subject with and for the graduate students of the Center for Global Change and Governance at Rutgers-Newark. Neither they nor the Center would be there if it had not been for the vision and support of Norman Samuels and Harvey Feder, Provost and Assistant Provost of the Rutgers-Newark Campus. Finally, I would like to express my gratitude to Queen Beatrix of the Netherlands and the Royal Palace Foundation of Amsterdam for the invitation to deliver a lecture on topics discussed in this book in Amsterdam in October 1998 – an invitation which proved to be an important stimulus in writing this book.

Preface

Globalization, particularly in its role as the motor of global capitalism and global markets, has become a very common expression. It can be used to explain both new opportunities and new tensions and anxieties; it can be called in justification of political action and inaction and it can appear to explain everything yet nothing. This study takes a longer look at the various elements which make up both the contemporary fact and the ongoing processes of globalization, placing them in the flow of history and explaining their contemporary context. It begins by explaining what globalization is and why it has happened. The following chapters then deal, first, with its effects on the global economy, through the emergence of global markets and the changing patterns of global companies and, secondly, on national governments and their shifting responsibilities. The third chapter examines the unfolding changes in the machinery of global relationships, ranging from the foreign policies of states to the sharply rising significance of new players on the global stage. These tend to be private rather than public, though they are increasingly mixed, and deal with environmental, humanitarian and human rights issues. The effects of the increasing power of global economic entities on global politics and the significance of contemporary variations in the patterns of peace and war are included in the discussion. The book ends with an assessment of what conclusions can be drawn as to likely outcomes in the future and to what extent they can be persuaded to be beneficial rather than destructive.

There are five significant themes running through this book. The first is perhaps the most straightforward: globalization has been brought about by an evolving communications revolution which has a continuous history from the invention of the steam locomotive to the Internet. There were, of course, previous important advances in communications made at different times in different parts of the world. But the real beginning of the globalizing process came when the steam locomotive revolutionized the transport of people, goods and information, particularly newspapers, and, at much the same time, the electric telegraph first divorced verbal communication from whatever was the speed of terrestrial transport. The point at which telecommunications development ceased to serve the old dispensations of human governance and began to threaten them, came as the ironic result of their own efforts to save themselves in the event of a nuclear holocaust. The resulting creation of a self-propelled, continuous, global, computer-controlled information system escaped from the purely military domain first into use by scientific research and thence into the hands of individual human beings. It is they and not their governments who have been empowered and nothing has been the same since.

The second theme is the profound effects of a developing contrast between the shape of globalized activities as they are evolving and the structures of human commerce and governance which remain with us from the past. The institutions of the national state and the way in which states have related to each other, paralleled by the similar shapes of industrial concerns and the companies that own them, have been essentially vertical or pyramidal in shape. The political and commercial landscape has been filled with tall structures, hierarchically arranged internally, territorially defined and communicating with each other only from their apexes. The arrangement, particularly from the end of the nineteenth century when the scope and powers of national governments sharply increased, became highly schematized, almost baroque in its strictly controlled ornamentation, so that the systems both in domestic and international politics became ends in themselves, the objects both of admiration and political ambition.

Thirdly, the coming of globalized activities on the back of an evolving communications revolution has produced a new characteristic shape. These activities are mainly conducted by individual human beings, who thereby escape from traditional hierarchies, have no limits imposed by geography or time of day and thus no necessary territorial element and can occur outside the political control of national governments. What is happening occurs horizontally across the world. The effect is to produce many different overlapping plates of activity, global markets and other forms of e-trading, entertainment and leisure interests of every kind, news and information – the variety is such that no complete list could ever be made. This layering of plates of different activities is in itself a highly complicated development and is producing some risky and exciting relationships within itself. What it is also doing is to create some very colourful short circuits within the pre-existing structures as new horizontal activities flood in, seep into their foundations and in some cases partly immerse them. This mixture of shapes and the consequential tensions and confusions between them is the principal reason why the contemporary world seems so strange, why pulling familiar political and economic levers or pressing well-used switches may either produce little or no result or a very unexpected one. Wholly new relationships of power, administration and political activity have to be arrived at in order to make sense of the combinations we have both created and inherited.

It is a further theme of this book that this is not an entirely new task. The situation itself is unprecedented in its details and is remarkably separated from past political and economic evolutions by its speed, and qualitatively in the nature of the activities that it has made possible. However, to have a world in which it is evident that the sources of power and consequentially its distribution are on the move is not new. Nor is it new that human societies find the exercise of power over them unacceptable unless parallel means are found to control and limit its use. It is possible to learn much from observing the circumstances in which the last major change of this kind occurred some 300 years ago when the territorially sovereign state began to emerge in Europe, subsequently to spread across the world. Knowing how the structures we have in place emerged is useful information when they are under threat and need to be reconceived. Understanding what they supplied in terms of creating public acceptance that power must be exercised – political legitimacy – is even more crucial when the contemporary task is to reconstruct that acceptance in new circumstances; and, more than that, to make it fit with what will remain of the old. The problem has many dimensions and they are discussed in Chapter 2; here, however, is one way of expressing it practically. The currency markets have become globalized. The efforts of national governments to manipulate or control these markets have now become fruitless, whether by a government whose currency is under speculative pressure or by other governments seeking to support it. The consequences for individual human beings, never mind whole societies, of what the currency markets do can be totally devastating, headily enriching or anything in between. In the past, people expected their governments to protect them from the worst effects of economic change either by using various forms of economic policy or by arranging cushioning through social services, or usually both. People, to differing degrees in different traditions and regimes, exercised some measure of control over their governments – by electoral processes at best, or by revolutions at worst. There was therefore a connection between important government policy reactions to economic conditions and the opinions of the society concerned. In the contemporary case that link has been broken: who ever elected a currency speculator? More than that, who has ever elected the heads or officials of the IMF or the World Bank, the only organizations who have some kind of role to play, however decreasingly effective that role is becoming?

It is a fourth theme of this book that there is inherent in this situation a related problem to be solved. It is easy enough to suggest that what is required is a kind of global extension of democracy; that the contemporary sources of horizontally operating power and authority should in some way be democratized. Apart from the intellectual and administrative difficulty of separating democracy from the essentially territorial basis from which it emerged, there is another serious gap to be filled. The idea of representation both in political systems and in the diplomatic relations between states has been a crucial element in constructing political legitimacy. That was how it became possible to find and speak to the representative of a particular source of power or authority. But it was a prior condition of doing this that the authority in question had itself evolved a physical structure capable of appointing a credible representative. In the case of currency speculators, or most other activities now being pursued globally, there are as yet no effective structures which could send forth representatives. It is simply not going to be possible to create means of controlling global sources of power by democratic or any other means until there are adequate representative bodies or persons to talk to. Neither censure, continuous monitoring nor encouragement can be operated by being sent into cyberspace, hoping that some individual operator's better nature will respond. Where we are with this problem is further discussed in Chapter 3.

The fifth theme underlies the others. The problems that globalization has brought look more serious at present than the extraordinary economic prospects that also beckon. But the second will not follow without some resolution of the first. The risk of failure in the global markets and the risk of political and social violence in the face of uncontrolled power, weakened national governments and a globally unequal distribution of economic benefits, are both deadly serious. It is a major argument of this book that if the extraordinary and often contradictory conditions that human society is now experiencing are to be managed successfully, there must be a broad understanding of what is happening, why it is happening and what direction events are most likely to take. This book is intended to be a contribution to that process. Only on this basis can general political judgements be made about what is inexorable and not worth resisting and those areas where intelligent management can make real choices and thus take decisions which will help to make what is not inevitable as acceptable as possible. The future security of human society depends upon getting such judgements right.

This book is not intended to be a full academic study, though students may find it useful as a base camp from which to climb to more advanced and detailed studies; nor does it seek to simplify what is complex and often contradictory. It sets out a single, coherent, steadily unfolding account expressed as clearly as the material will allow. It challenges the interested reader to think about the fact and the problems of globalization in ways that may not be familiar and anticipates that such readers will view the world rather differently in the future. Those who work in the markets, in globally operating companies, in governments, in international institutions, those who write about them in the media, as well as those who are formally students and teachers in the relevant disciplines, may, I hope, from time to time see themselves individually as if in a mirror. But I hope even more that they may also reflect on how best we may handle the biggest single entity the human race has ever had in its hands before – because globalization really has delivered up the world – and share our reflections with as many other people as possible.

1
Introduction: the Origins and Significance of Globalization

Why should we make a special effort to understand globalization? There are two important reasons: the process and the results of globalization are changing the way we live our lives on a personal basis and they are changing the institutions which we collectively use to give form and predictability to our economic, social and political relationships. The second reason is that the word has become so widely used that it has taken on all sorts of levels of meaning which confuse rather than enlighten and constrain logical thinking about the exceedingly difficult problems that globalization has brought. To give an example: views about globalization have moved within a few years from seeing it as an irresistible lava flow, to assessing it as only one among many features of the contemporary world, to dismissing it as 'globaloney', yet still being capable of fearing it as 'globaphobia'. Plainly some straightening out is required, or we shall begin to feel like the speaker in Russell Mearns's nonsense poem:

> As I was going up the stair
> I met a man who wasn't there.
> He wasn't there again today;
> I wish, I wish, he'd stay away.

To begin at the beginning: what is globalization and why has it happened?

Globalization is the latest stage in a long accumulation of techno-logical advance which has given human beings the ability to con-duct their affairs across the world without reference to nationality, government authority, time of day or physical environment. These activities may be commercial, financial, religious, cultural, social or political; nothing is barred. Technological advances in global com-munications have made globalization possible; while the fact of globalization itself is to be seen in the contemporary surge in human activities conducted globally. The effects of these activities on the whole range of humanity's expectations, systems and struc-tures have been and are a heady mixture: they have come and keep coming at different paces in different places; sometimes they create entirely new significant activities, sometimes they share them with older systems and structures; sometimes they induce adaptation but sometimes they erode and destroy. They represent both opportuni-ties and threats. They are the subject of this book.

Globalization has happened because technological advances have broken down many physical barriers to worldwide communication which used to limit how much connected or cooperative activity of any kind could happen over long distances. Think what has hap-pened to a book, which, in its printed form, was the product of a previous cutting-edge technology. In addition to being a collection of atoms, a physical object usable only by individuals possessing copies, it can now become a collection of bytes, having no physical existence but usable by everyone connected to cyberspace. You have only to think of the limitations of the past to see how much has changed. American Indian smoke signals, Inca relay runners, French semaphores, English hilltop beacons and slow sailing ships in gen-eral all tell their stories of slow and cumbrous communications over distance. Compare that with the almost instant effect of contempo-rary faxes, e-mail and the Internet. This communications revolu-tion is the cause of globalization. The result of these technological advances has been a huge increase in human activities carried on without hindrance across the world; and these consequences are also often described as globalization, very obviously when politicians wish to find a useful explanation for action or inaction at particular moments. Thus globalization has come to mean both an ongoing process and a contemporary condition, the result of that process. Plainly the two things are intertwined, but it can be important to remember that the word has these two meanings. Both the process itself and its consequences are immensely important and we shall be discussing them; but to begin with we will concentrate on examining the process and its evolution – the causes of globalization.

Technological advances in communications have accelerated steadily since the early nineteenth century. There were earlier and important improvements such as the invention and development of the printing press in Western Europe – the Chinese also made the same discovery, but did not develop it – which enabled a far faster dissemination of ideas and information and had a crucial effect during the Renaissance and Reformation periods when the pace and depth of intellectual and political life was greatly extended. And there were improvements to sailing ships and the techniques of navigation which enabled long distance, but epically slow, sea journeys to begin. So technological improvements have always been important. But the age of continuous and rapid development in communications did not start, however, until the Industrial Revolution had accomplished its first stage in Great Britain and the age of steam had truly begun. Thereafter, three stages of development followed. The first was the longest and flowed from the combined effects of applying the steam engine to land and sea transport and the invention and installation worldwide of the electric telegraph. The second, which began during the Second World War, was also a combination. The perfecting of rocket propulsion led to the ability to launch orbiting satellites. This, when there were enough of them and when combined with the previous invention of the telephone, gave a global and reliable communications coverage. The role of the telephone, hitherto somewhat restricted to short or at best medium distance use, was thus transformed into the major communications channel. The third stage, following rapidly in the 1970s, applied the computer, itself transformed in speed, volume and efficiency by the evolution of the microchip, as both manager and transmitter of the system. The Internet was the result.

The first stage began with the application of the steam engine to land transport. The first attempts to fit it into a road running machine failed, often explosively. But in the 1820s, Robert Stephenson succeeded in fitting an engine into a vehicle that ran on rails. The notion that railways made moving heavy goods easier, whether by human energy as used in mines, or horsepower, as applied to lines between mines and wharves, had already become familiar, so the marriage of steam with rail was not in principle difficult to arrange. It was instantly effective, raised the speed of transport by a factor of five even in its earliest development, spread very rapidly in Europe, North America and India and at once began to have revolutionary effects.

There were three principal consequences: first, industrial. The railway created an infrastructure industry of its own and it greatly accelerated and expanded the scope of other industrial activities. Secondly, the railway hugely increased the amount, the speed and the conceivable geographical range of transporting goods and people; thirdly, the railway carried news, technical information, questions and replies far faster than had hitherto been imaginable. At around the same time, another technological breakthrough accelerated written communication even more dramatically than the railway had done: the electric telegraph. Pretty primitive short-distance telegraphing by means of flags was already in use, particularly for military signalling and messages of the simplest kind – just 'danger', for example, had been achieved by the use of bonfires on top of lighthouses placed strategically on coasts. Transmitting electrically by wire and using symbols for encoding and decoding the message divorced the technique from any relationship to the speed of land transport. At its most dramatic, it could, provided it worked well and was not interrupted by ignorant handling or civil strife en route, cut the time it took to send a message from London to Peking from three months to three minutes. The combination was potent. At its most blatant, the possession of both railways and the telegraph put into the hands of government the ability to learn quickly what was happening at the edges of its territory, dispatch troops and/or officials in response to that information by train. They could then be told what to do when they reached their destination by telegraph, a command which could be adjusted in the light of the latest news both from the distant point and at the administrative centre.

The kind of society over which newly empowered governments presided was also changed by speeded-up internal communications. The railway, the telegraph, eventually the automobile and the telephone created both national markets satisfied by national suppliers and nationally shared news provided by national newspapers. This had the effect of 'branding' a society both informally and formally with shared cultural and commercial symbols which marked it clearly and distinguished it from others. The coming of the railways even required the imposition of an agreed national time, or time zones, depending on size, a fact which explains why British national time was for a long time called 'railway time'. The emergence of much larger areas of coherent social and political polities which the railways made possible was a primary cause of the emergence of fully national politics in the later nineteenth century, accompanied by the emergence of mass political parties, using the national press to promote a highly simplified and sloganized form of political debate. The result was to promote even further the sense of national differences. The vertical divisions between state structures were emphasized and created an internal alignment between what technology had enabled governments to do and what their peoples therefore wished from them, thus further cementing the political bond between government and governed.

The most striking, and eventually violently destructive, effect of these developments was that they increased the potential size of a state in a very dramatic way. Since the seventeenth century, a pattern of steadily increasing power and authority in rulers and governments had developed. This was first driven by the fact that governments which ruled as efficiently as the contemporary situation made possible were more secure both internally and externally. During the eighteenth century in Europe, the connection between reasonable efficiency and the power of a state settled into an observable optimum size and what determined that size was the ease with which the total territory of a ruler could be coherently governed. And that ease was in turn related to a contemporary speed of communication which linked the centre to the periphery in not more than about five days' travel. States that were bigger could not be efficiently ruled and those that were smaller suffered from insufficient basic resources. The contemporary optimum thus arrived at turned out to be roughly the size of France. Over time, as the speed of communications increased, what was optimum also increased. Much of international politics and warfare was fundamentally the result of changes in this condition from the late seventeenth century until the last part of the nineteenth.

Much of the domestic political turmoil of the period was also a result of such changes, though here the question was related but different. Basically the more significant the activity of government became, the more significant a role those who conducted it played in the lives of those they ruled. Populations understandably began to want to be sure that so much power and influence was subject to perceptible controls, sufficient to control potential abuses. This meant that intense struggles both philosophical and real developed about how to arrive at an acceptable framework for government, which on the one hand allowed that it had to exist in an effective way, but on the other set limits to its power. The outcome of these internal struggles will be assessed in Chapter 2.

The expansion of the territorial area over which government and administration could be effective benefited two states in particular: the United States and the Russian Empire, subsequently the Soviet Union. They already possessed great land mass, and once they had installed the new mechanisms of communication could expect to enjoy the advantages in resources, demography and strategy that great size conferred. The United States moved much more rapidly than Russia, but both were visibly becoming actually or potentially globally dominant by the turn of the twentieth century. In the case of Imperial Russia, even facing the 1905 Revolution, it was the potentiality that mattered: Germany for example was not lulled into any sense of security and never took her eyes off Russia's industrial and armaments capacity. For states overtaken by these changes, new problems of security, both economic and strategic, began to intrude. Two states, Germany in Europe and Japan in Asia, who had benefited from late and, therefore relatively advanced, industrial revolutions, became very powerful in their regions, but could not advance further unless they added to their restricted land mass. Plainly the temptation to capitalize on short-term regional predominance to make sufficient territorial gains to even up the balance with the USA and Russia would be very strong; and in fact it proved irresistible. From the late nineteenth century onward this factor began to overtake in importance the more familiar patterns of inter-state competition, which Lenin had identified as capitalism and imperialism. For just about 100 years, from 1895 to 1990, the optimum size which contemporary communications systems had imposed dominated the direction world politics took. Attempts by Japan and Germany to expand their territory were successfully resisted by the USA and Russia until, after 1955, the year of the Geneva Conference which both President Eisenhower and General Secretary Khruschev attended in person, the two great land mass states achieved a kind of balance between them which expressed itself in the sterile stability of the Cold War years.

This outcome in international politics became the chief propellant of the next phase in the advancing technology of global communications. It was to rejoin in a crucial way the two paths of development which had become separated since the invention of the electric telegraph. The telegraph had made the transmission of messages and information independent of the techniques of land, sea and eventually air transport. Improved railways, improved ships, the invention of the automobile and the achievement of human flight in its ever-increasing speed and efficiency pushed along human and commercial mobility both in speed and quantity and is still doing so. We are now promised flights from London to Sydney in three hours and we can already see the effects of the sheer numbers of people who move about the planet by plane. This is a world in which the ecology itself is troubled by eco-tourism. The separate and independent path taken by communications added cables to telegraph lines, the telephone to cables and the radio telephone to the telephone and moved from coding messages to the transmission of voice conversation. As it turned out, the two tracks were to be reunited by military technology: the development of the jet engine during the Second World War, followed by the first successful production and use of a rocket weapon – the V2 – by Germany towards the end of the war, and by the refinement of the computer in the second half of the twentieth century.

When the USA and the USSR began their military competition after the defeat of Germany and Japan, they capitalized on the developments achieved during the Second World War and refined them. They were soon able to improve the delivery of nuclear weapons by using rockets, and by doing so greatly improved the power and range of missiles that they were able to create the intercontinental ballistic missile. The technological advances thus gained became available for launching satellites into and orbiting them within the earth's immediate inner space. Soviet man orbited the earth, American man went to the moon and both types of men learnt how to inspect and spy on each other by using satellites of ever-increasing sophistication. The communications that could be made from and to satellites turned out to have even more significance than their intelligence capabilities and ended, among other things, by transforming the role of the telephone.

The telephone was invented by Alexander Graham Bell in 1876 and much improved by Thomas Edison in the 1890s. It solved some of the problems of carrying voice messages which the telegraph had not been able to do. It remained, however, linked to a land line for nearly 100 years and no effective undersea cable relay telephone link – for example between the USA and Europe – was installed until the 1950s. The result was that the telephone remained an essentially local convenience, particularly in urban areas. Long-distance or international calling remained rare, with connections often difficult to establish and then it could be hard to hear the other caller distinctly or reliably. What rapidly increased the usefulness of the telephone was the divorce from land or undersea lines, which radio had not been able to achieve satisfactorily, but which the combination of the computer and the orbiting satellite made possible. Once there were enough satellites continuously orbiting the earth, a global telephone relay service could be created. The first such service began in 1969 and, using microwaves rather than radio waves, provided the opportunity for the development of global communications using telephone conversations, TV programmes, high-speed digital data and facsimile pictures. At the same time, the old limitations on the quantity of traffic which land lines had imposed were almost dissolved.

The line of evolution which led from the jet engine to the launching of satellites met and joined up with another line of technological advance. This, too, owed much for its rapid development to the strategic imperatives of the Cold War. There were two major considerations. Developing computers, particularly through the introduction of the microchip and the ending of the use and storage of inefficient and cumbrous tapes, was an important adjunct to the management and control of technologically advanced weapons and equipment. The second was the need to develop a means of maintaining information stores and communications systems in the event and aftermath of a nuclear war. Having been given accelerated development under these pressures, the commercial and administrative application of the modern computer was naturally rapid and, like the steam engine, its effect both on manufacturing industry generally and in creating a whole new industry in itself has had profound consequences. Nor has its effect been confined to industry. It has also revolutionized the conduct of financial and investment business as well as ordinary daily domestic life.

From the point of view of global communications, the development of digital information transfers was the technological advance that mattered most. This advance emerged from the need to safeguard information and systems in the event of nuclear attack and followed from the realization that in order to send data, which is more sensitive to circuitry distortion than the human voice, it should be transmitted digitally if it is to be both quick and reliable. It also became clear that whereas in the early days of computer involvement its principal use was as a tool to keep increasingly complicated systems up and running, the future required that the computer should act as the actual transmitting device itself. In 1962, at MIT, the first steps were taken to bring these developments together and the idea of sending data digitally in packets was born. In 1966 at the Defense Advanced Research Projects Agency the mechanism for putting this principle to work on computer networks was designed and the first form of the contemporary Internet, ARPANET (Advanced Research Projects Agency Network) was planned and published in 1967. While this was going on, the RAND Corporation had been working on something very similar for military purposes, and in the UK the National Physical Laboratory had also come up with and introduced the term 'packets'. All three originators contributed to the actual construction of ARPANET. The new network was a combination of computer hard- and software used to compress messages into packets and send them over the telephone line. To make the system more broadly available further simplifications had to be made, but with the World Wide Web and the emergence of search engines, the Internet as we know it became possible. It represented the completion of the junction between the telephone facilities offered by the orbiting satellite, as well as existing ground based networks, and the computer networked system developed by ARPANET.

The intersection of these paths, which was so significant for the development of a totally globalized telecommunications system, came in the 1970s and the result was the heady mixture available to us today: faxes, e-mail and the full panoply of Internet activity involving the provision and exchange of information and views, electronic commercial transactions and entertainment. There can be no doubt that this was a revolution, but it was still a revolution with limitations – not of scale but of quantity. The telephone/satellite link was not adequate to carry the traffic that developed: put in more contemporary terms there was not enough bandwidth. The solution to this problem has come in very recent times with the invention and installation of the fibre-optic cable: it is being laid under the world's oceans and will soon be available to every household in highly developed societies. There is as yet no sign where its limits may be and the traffic it can carry will ensure the continuation of the modern communications revolution into the foreseeable future.

These systems have produced a communications revolution at least the equal of that yielded by the train/telegraph combination and with equally momentous consequences. The first phase, playing out during the nineteenth century, altered the scope of human economic and political activity and created a global distribution of power among states: in doing so, it significantly increased the power and security of the USA and Russia and eventually relatively reduced the power of others. It did not, however, change the name of the game: the scope of government of every size and description was increased and they maintained supervision or control over all the instruments of communication. This remained true during the essentially military-driven second phase, serving the needs of the Cold War. The third and most recent phase, however, dominated by modern computer technology, has put the instruments of communication above and beyond the control of governments – such technology was, after all, designed to withstand a nuclear war which governments themselves were deemed unlikely to do – and created a network which serves individual human beings and their activities rather than specific societies and their authorities. In a nutshell, it is activities rather than traditional governmental authorities which have been the beneficiaries. Many previously important, even formerly vital, systems of administration – political, economic and social – have been rendered increasingly redundant as a result. It may well also turn out that future historians will attribute the end of the Cold War, at least in part, to the emergence of a self-propelling and universal communications system.

All governments whether large or small have been to some extent bypassed by these events, and we shall discuss the internal effects of this in the second chapter. The international consequences have also been momentous. The advantages that the first phase gave to the great land mass states have been withdrawn, but this time there have been no successors. The second phase has not transferred power and security to a different optimum size of state, so much as move them away from existing states of any sort. It may, but we do not yet know, lead to the complete reconstruction of the institutions of human society. If it does so, then the likely pattern will be one of large-scale, global activities, generating their own styles of management and authority, accompanied by small-scale geographically described local mechanisms, as small or smaller than existing provincial structures, designed to accomplish the basic minimum of local government. These are the circumstances which importantly help to explain both the collapse of the Soviet Union and the puzzling weakness which seems to affect the USA in its lonely role as only remaining superpower. What had once propelled their rise to global dominance and then sustained them both no longer does so: the USSR, which was inherently more divided, internally fell to pieces and may have further falling yet to do; the USA, which was essentially a unitary structure, survived but sits uncomfortably in such a changed environment, uncertain how to behave. This is chiefly because such predominance arrived suddenly and unexpectedly, after a period of considerable self-doubt, and, even more difficult to interpret, because predominance itself has lost a clear meaning: predominant over what exactly or whom?

The best way of thinking about these changes is to imagine the organizational structures of the past, whether commercial and economic or political, as functioning vertically. They operated up and down and narrowed at the top like a pyramid. They related to each other from the top and regarded each other as separate systems, having individual characteristics, particularly, for example, in economic policies and political organization and generally expected that their relationships would be competitive and adversarial, sinking from time to time into actual conflict. Advantages were sometimes anticipated to flow from cooperative arrangements, particularly where convenience for all would come from generally accepted administrative norms, for example in matters of disease control or the regulation of international commercial traffic. This kind of cooperation led to the appearance of inter-governmental organizations which gave a more complicated texture to their relationships from the end of the nineteenth century. But however much the texture was complicated either by international organizations or by the emergence of multinational companies, there was a complete expectation that, at the end of the day, final authority lay with governments and the decisions that they took at the apex of their particular structure.

This vertically structured and territorially arranged system of government has been pushed over by the advent of the most recent communications revolution. Some of the most important human activities and exchanges now cross these vertical divisions with complete ease. This penetration is not achieved by some kind of victorious advance but by using technological changes in communications systems to ignore such vertical divisions. They are thus happening across the globe on a horizontal basis, without reference to territorial location, time of day or local political and legal authority. They are able to do so because the use of the fax, e-mail and the Internet takes place without either the permission of governments or the need to pay dues to them. Relationships can be global or local in scope entirely at will: question, answer, information and command can pass instantly across the globe. Financial exchanges and stock market trading have become continuous activities operating like a global horizontal plate, interacting with other plates similarly arranged, for example, industrial and manufacturing businesses. These now locate themselves where it is most advantageous to undertake any particular part of their operation and create alliances with other firms as is most appropriate. This process, which has many other ramifications, has fundamentally impaired the ability of governments to run independent macroeconomic policies and reduced most of them to micromanagement designed to ensure that they create the optimum conditions for attracting global investment to their own area. This is not sovereignty in any recognizable sense, it is a form of servanthood – serving the needs of one of the most important horizontal plates of global activity but, nonetheless, it also represents a new and significant role for the state to play. We will take a closer look at these effects in the next section.

The effects of horizontally arranged global activities are not confined to political, economic and commercial operations. There have been notable cultural consequences as well. In this field, as in others, the communications revolution has worked at both the broadest and the narrowest level, tending to squeeze the familiar middle. The ubiquity of the Internet has the effect of confirming and extending the spread of the English language in its North American form and with it the culture of the United States, and, to a much lesser extent of the United Kingdom. This last is derived to some extent from the extraordinary global use that is made of the radio and now television services of the BBC. What had been spread as the language of two successive economic and political hegemonies has become the language of global communication, operating horizontally and independently of the views and intentions of its progenitors. This is one reason why attempts by both the French and the Chinese to limit its spread have failed and will continue to fail. The predominance of English is not a political projection, but a matter of convenience. It is extremely fortunate that the language itself is so welcoming to neologism and grammatically plastic and that its literary tradition is so rich and powerful. Nonetheless, other cultural features of the English-speaking world have not proved to be universally welcome. Its association with moral degradation, as liberal attitudes may seem to some, with Christianity in various forms and with the propagation of the ideas associated with democracy are all offensive in some degree and in different places. The combination of rapid change leading to a sense of unfamiliarity, rootlessness and dismay is emphasized by the decline of traditional political structures. A sense of aggressive and implacable 'westernization' at the hands of a dominant global culture contributes to the rise of religious fundamentalisms and other forms of suspicious backlash, sometimes terrorist in form. Conspiracies of every kind, religious oddities, many predicting the end of the world and various versions of violently extreme political views all populate the Internet and gain global exposure thereby. A paradox then emerges in which the fundamentalist response seems very particularly ungrateful and even dangerous to those who deeply believe that they are only purveying things that are good in an equally fundamental sense.

Away from the global stresses of an unfolding convergent culture, the contemporary communications network encourages the pursuit of highly local and particularist activities. Small societies can propagate their own individual approaches to all cultural media and thus provide reliable focuses for daily life. Sometimes these represent a revival of older provincial loyalties, submerged in the process of forming larger states. Particular skills and activities, always a focus for loyalty and association on a small geographical scale, can now achieve a wider participation and enthusiasms of every kind have received a kind of shot in the arm from the ease of global contact with the like-minded. So have less satisfactory activities: transnational crime has become a growth industry, particularly in the field of financial fraud and money laundering, as has the provision of undesirable information – on pornographic networks, for example, and how to make terrorist weapons, including chemical and biological ones. All in all, the Internet has empowered smaller groups following sometimes micro-enthusiams and skills as much as it has furthered a macro-predominance of English and English-based culture on a global basis; however, both these effects weaken rather than enhance the older forms of loyalties and expectation based on medium-sized societies organized in the more traditional state form.

In this introductory chapter, we have identified the processes which have induced the worldwide connectivity which we often call globalization. We have also touched on some of the consequences which are themselves often called globalization so that cause and effect can be distinguished. Chapter 2 will concentrate more closely on the effects, first chiefly economic and the second chiefly political and cultural.

2
Societies, Governments and the Global Economy

2.1 Global capitalism, global markets, national governments and global entities, private and public

In Chapter 1, we discussed the causes and the eventual arrival of globalization. In section 2.2 we shall investigate its political, social and cultural consequences – its effects on governments and peoples. This first section will be concerned with the chief economic and financial issues involved, because they underlie the others and because they have become the most obvious way in which the results of globalization present themselves to individual people. Of course, it is artificial to divide things up in this manner: many factors rub against each other simultaneously and throughout we are dealing with an unfolding process – unfinished business. We must begin at the most fundamental level: the latest phase in the continuing revolutions in the technology of global communications, which in one guise or another date back to the sixteenth century in Europe, have created a new situation – not just a further stage in an evolutionary process, but something different in kind.

What has made this so, and one important way in which contemporary globalization is different from the emergence of the globally interdependent economy of around 1900, is the fundamental fact that the routine use of global communication has passed out of the sole control or regulation of governments and companies. Ordinary people have joined the club. This has meant that the relationship between individual human beings can now become direct and horizontally expressed across the world: it is their activities, and not their authorities, who are the new beneficiaries. The process is far from complete – there are more people in the world who do not have access to the Internet than there are those who do, but the activities of those who do have become so compellingly important that a general revolution has occurred. One of the chief characteristics of this revolution is that it is yielding highly contradictory results. At the most basic level, there is a growing contradiction between the huge benefits enjoyed by those who are wired and the loss of opportunity enforced on those who are not. Another contradiction is that the creation of a single world based on an integrated and comprehensive communications system creates pressures and opportunities both felt and requiring to be managed at a global level. But, on the other hand, the fact that this system also has the effect of giving new opportunities to individuals and small groups, either pursuing particular interests or belonging to a particular geographical region, has given a whole new influence and significance to the needs and feelings of people operating at a local level. Those most affected by this situation happen to be the forms of organization and government with which we are most familiar – large companies, national states and associations of states: they are being squeezed in the middle of the new dispensation. This effect has important implications for the future governance of the world, as we shall see in section 2.2. It also has effects on global markets, the economic policy role of governments and the structure of multinational organizations.

At the end of the twentieth century, it looks clear that there has been a kind of triumph of global capitalism. The emergence of a larger number of states almost universally pursuing market-oriented policies accompanied by liberalization and deregulation has produced a remarkable platform of shared attitudes and policies. The reduction of barriers to cross-border transactions and the deregulation and privatization of a variety of domestic markets have been significant. For example, between 1991 and 1997 of 151 countries reported by the United Nations Conference on Trade and Development (UNCTAD) to have made changes to their internal regimes, 135 introduced fewer regulations and only 16 increased them. This is not to say that different societies and geographical areas do not pursue different forms of capitalism: they plainly do. Malaysia's is not the same as Argentina's, to take two widely separated examples.

Nor has every society embraced the market with full-hearted assent. The Russian Federation is an outstanding example of pervasive doubt about the benefits of global capitalism, as it is equally an example of the apparent impossibility of a government escaping from it. But the sense that the global economic system shares more than just an instant and ever-ready connectivity is strong.

It is possible to list the most significant features of global capitalism. Cross-border transactions have become deeper, more extensive and more interconnected than ever before. Resources, capabilities, goods and services have become more mobile than ever before. Multinational enterprises create and disseminate more wealth and they originate and produce in more countries than ever before. One result is increasing real and financial volatility in cross-border markets – particularly obvious in capital and currency markets. The character of cross-border transactions, particularly in services, has been permanently changed by the digital environment and the onset of e-commerce. This last is plainly on the brink of a major expansion, beginning with intra-business transactions. Private personal use has been slower to take off. In addition to these consequences of the spatial widening which the technological basis of globalization has brought, global capitalism has other distinctive features.

The technological advances in communications have vastly increased the significance of the economic asset represented by *knowledge* and downgraded the importance of *things* in the global economy. This shift has been the chief motor of contemporary development. A computing skill may be more valuable than auto engines or knives and forks. This is partly because of the needs of the system itself: to use it, operate it, administer it and improve it has evoked both a new area of highly technical knowledge and a new manufacturing industry to support it. But it is also, importantly, because the very existence of the system makes the dissemination of all forms of knowledge more or less immediate. Knowledge no longer has a territorial location in terms of access or use. It does, however, still do so in respect of training and education, with highly advantageous effects – if most likely quite temporary, since equalization is already beginning to occur – on those areas where they are available. In all cases and in all places, it puts a revolutionary pressure on the character, purpose and timing of education, giving it for the first time fully global norms to meet.

A further notable feature is that although the production of many enterprises, particularly multinationals, spreads across the globe, a greater concentration of some kinds of economic activity has appeared both between and within some countries than has occurred before. Finally, all forms of alliances and cooperative ventures, within and between firms, between governments and between firms and non-market institutions have become more important elements in the global economic system than before.

The result of this has been to complete the emergence of a global economy. In addition to the empowerment of individuals, the spatial change is significant and different from the fully interdependent global economy which has become familiar in the twentieth century. The comparison is interesting. At the end of the twentieth century, both the similarities and differences of circumstances are striking compared with those experienced 100 years ago. Both periods show common characteristics: widespread and dramatic technological change; a new generation of telecommunications advances shrinking the boundaries of economic activity; a state of flux in the organizational structures and managerial strategies of firms; a realignment of the geography of economic and political power. Then, as now, the jurisdiction of nation states was entering a new era and civic responsibilities were being redefined and new relationships were being forged between, and within, private and public institutions, and among different religious and ethnic groups. But, nonetheless, the differences are more marked than these similarities. Most obvious is that while the globalizing economic tendencies of the early twentieth century were taking place within a well-established and widely accepted social, economic and political order, today's revolution challenges long-established ideologies and values, and, indeed, the very institutional fabric of society, more as the creation of great industrial conurbations did during the earlier phases of the Industrial Revolution. And there is no clear guide to the pattern of future developments. Contemporary developments may divide individuals and institutions as much as unify them and the hierarchical capitalism which created wealth for 100 years looks vulnerable.

Transnational flows of capital, goods, services, technology and information have now acquired a speed, intensity, comprehensive and self-reinforcing relevance and fully global reach that make them qualitatively different from their precursors of even recent decades. Figures for foreign direct investment, foreign trade and foreign portfolio investment make the point perfectly clear. Foreign direct investment (Fdi), as a proportion of world gross product rose from 7.8 per cent in 1967 to 14 per cent in 1988 and to 21.4 per cent in 1996. The value of cross-border mergers and acquisitions rose dramatically from $25 billion in 1980 to $350 billion in 1996. The annual average percentage growth of world trade rose from 4 per cent between 1853 and 1913 to 6 per cent between 1950 and 1985 and then to 7.5 per cent between 1985 and 1996. Trade between firms rose from 10 per cent to 40 per cent between 1960 and 1996. Foreign portfolio investment rose 14 times between 1970 and 1996. In earlier conditions, different economic units or blocs or states could not completely evade the effects of what was going on in the others, and were inextricably linked in a financial system based on the 'single currency' of the Gold Standard. During the Great Depression of the 1930s, it was discovered that attempting a controlled economic isolation failed to work and during the postwar period, the capitalist world moved gradually but with increasing speed towards the general deregulation of the 1980s. The implosion of the communist bloc after 1989 globalized the pursuit of basically capitalist economic policy, though causing some parallel economic collapses while doing so: in Ukraine, for example. The effect has been called the triumph of global capitalism. The triumph of global capitalism has not, however, been solely the result of the collapse of communism, nor, looking at it from another angle, was the collapse of communism solely caused by the advance of global capitalism, as will be seen in the next section. Fully global capitalism has also needed the effects of the contemporary communications revolution to come into existence.

Global markets

This can clearly be seen in the emergence of the global markets – in stocks, in currencies, in banking – and in the changing structures of multinational entities. Stock markets, as the events of 1929–30 showed vividly enough, have been both interconnected and only unreliably amenable to government policies or decisions for some time. But at that time, they remained territorial and separate, vertical structures communicating with each other across global space with reasonable but not perfect ease. The number of individuals involved in their operations both as investors and operators was comparatively small. The de-territorialized global stock market created by total global communications is a different beast. The number of individuals involved, particularly as investors, has risen sharply and neither the time of day nor the physical location of an investor matters much at all. Access to cyberspace from anywhere on the globe will allow personal and instantaneous participation in the global stock market. The fate of single state economies is affected by the movements of the markets, but the fate of individual investors can be affected even more. And that in turn de-territorializes the influence of stockholders on companies, their policies, investment decisions and ultimate fate. In short, the market in which companies generate capital has become global – that does not mean that all parts of the globe take part, but it does mean that all parts of the globe are potential sources of investment. It also means that all parts of the globe are potential objects of investment – a development which we will return to shortly. The single most important short-term effect of this is that the global stock market has become highly volatile; the umbilical cord that connected it to 'real' economic activity has been broken and the extent that governments could, either by domestic policy measures or by combined action, attempt to control it has been reduced to almost nothing. The global stock market now presents itself as a leviathan, yet an unexpectedly capricious and nimble one.

Capriciousness is also a compelling characteristic of another important global market place. Currency speculation has for long been a difficult area for governments. They have from time to time been able to bring off temporary, but always welcome, victories against attacks upon particular currencies. But they have generally lacked success and their failure has been largely to do with the fact that currency speculation was related to some basic changes in the real economic situation in the currency area in question. What has now emerged is a 'virtual' market unamenable to government activity – cooperative or singular – and to a large degree unrelated to real economic conditions. There is no doubting the size of the shift. Since 1979, the turnover in the foreign exchange markets has risen to $1.5 trillion each day, 12 times the level of 1979 and over 50 times that of world trade. The effects on societies and individuals can be either catastrophic or enriching, but the circumstances are equally volatile.

The global flows of capital moving round the world at more than a trillion dollars a day are routed through the global banking system. Here, too, a formerly cooperative and understood set of arrangements between effective banks operating vertically in relation both to each other and to particular economic areas has been undermined by the emergence of a global economy. The size of the world banking market as a percentage of world gross output rose from 1.2 per cent in 1964 to 45 per cent in 1994. This quantity of capital flooding round the globe looking for the most advantageous temporary destination has become a frequently quixotic economic activity, an end in itself, not necessarily the servant of physically located real economic action expressed as factories, goods and services leading to employment and commerce. Global banking operates increasingly as a single unit, not an interdependent system. It thus functions without familiar landmarks and includes areas without any tradition of free domestic, let alone international, banking, and the result has been chaotic mixtures of sometimes little understood and recently installed domestic arrangements coming under pressure from a global system, itself at sea in uncharted waters. The result is further volatility, to match those arising in the stock markets and the currency markets. So serious has this problem become, that in 1999 the first serious efforts to gain control have begun to emerge from within the market through a mechanism derived from the Bank of International Settlements. It will be interesting to see how this interacts with the market on the one hand and national governments on the other.

It seems unlikely that the emergence of this situation is a temporary phenomenon, to be endured before we all return to normal conditions. Normal has now become global and while, as we have seen, the development of the new is proving hard, the adjustments required of the old are perhaps even harder. Even in the older economically interdependent world familiar since the end of the nineteenth century, it was a reasonable expectation that governments would and could fulfil an obligation to manage both the macro- and microeconomic policies of their state. That there were some limitations on what might be achievable against a cyclical economic movement was accepted; but that governments had the greatest role to play was simply assumed. The electoral rhetoric of parties assumed it, the propaganda of dictators equally assumed it and the actual policies of governments of every type acted upon it. The growth of multinational companies seemed in the 1960s particularly to dent it, but contrary to some expectations, never went further than that. How different the situation is now. Not only have national governments found themselves having to adjust to a serious loss of economic power, multinational companies have found themselves as subject to the effects of globalization as states, and have, in one sense, almost equally become victims.

What has produced this effect has chiefly been a substantial deterritorialization of the labour market. The basic change is simple: the global communications system is now so complete and so immediate that there is no necessary connection between the point of ownership of a company, the point of manufacture of its goods – in whole or in part – and the point of their sale. Indeed it is quite possible, even likely, that all these activities will in fact be globally spread and physically widely separated – ownership, manufacture and sale. With the onset of electronic consumer purchasing – still in its infancy – it will shortly be true that even the point of acquisition will be globalized. You may manufacture where it is cheapest and/or most convenient to do so, administer in the same way, buy and pay the bill similarly. The current obvious examples of the emergence of a global labour market are the almost wholesale departure of clothing manufacture to Asian sites, attracted by less regulated conditions and cheap labour and, secondly, the ability of Indian educated computer programmers to deal with the year 2K problem. This effectively transfers most of the work from the highly developed economies that most require it to India which in practice needs it somewhat less, but nonetheless profits greatly. Other forms of manufacture show similar signs and the trend towards highly subsidiarized operations in which quite small parts of a mechanism will be made on the opposite side of the world and then assembled in another different place under the management of a company physically based in yet another location, is significant in this regard. TVs, VCRs, fax machines and microwave ovens are all examples of this.

This is an example of a commonly observed contemporary phenomenon: the pressures are coming globally, but the response is often paradoxically local or regional. In economic terms this means that the conditions which an investing company regards as most attractive are likely to be set by factors which are highly localized: wage levels, environmental conditions, taxation, the educational level of the workforce, building standards. The smaller the state, the more these will be centrally controlled, but in larger states, they are generally part of the remit of regional government. A national government is seldom the best proprietor of a business park or a development area: subsidiarity, that is to say decisions taken at the lowest appropriate level, is generally applied. And since one region may see itself in competition with another for attracting external investment and thus employment, it may be powerfully motivated into supplying the desired conditions. Squeezed between the demands of the global economy and the response of its regions, the space in which national governments operate diminishes and even traditionally strongly unitary states find themselves devolving authority, willingly or unwillingly. They do so to units small enough to make the most effective and successful decisions in respect of attracting foreign direct investment to the region.

In very general terms the effects of all this have been favourable. For less developed societies in particular, globalization brings tremendous opportunities. It can bring employment and investment in hitherto unimaginable quantities and, perhaps in the longer term more significantly, it brings some levelling in comparative knowledge. What is globally accessible can be available to all and enables some remarkably rapid catching up to take place. Easily available capital and electronic information can be a kind of leveller, and, in less developed countries, they can level up. On the other hand, rapid expansion puts great strains on underdeveloped infrastructures, underdeveloped financial systems and inefficient domestic administration. The cumulative effect of this and concomitant often endemic corruption can lead to crises, as recently observed in Asia. For more developed societies, these factors may not apply, but the short-term effect, chiefly on employment, can be more damaging.

The role of national governments

In an age when the communications revolution has allowed manufacturing to be located anywhere on the globe, the role of a government, though it is reduced in terms of its macroeconomic decision-making capacity, remains significant, and is even enhanced in respect of the policies it adopts which create encouragement for global companies to locate part of their operation within its territory. The state does not disappear, but is downsized; so, too, are some companies in advanced societies. It is likely that workforces will be cheaper elsewhere and no less usable, and it is also likely that vastly improved communications will make the use of precisely focused small-scale suppliers more efficient than in-house provision – a particularly tough change to accept in the former communist world. So the number of smaller concerns rises and while the scope of larger ones may increase – by mega mergers, for example – the number of their employees falls. The amount of less skilled employment in the developed world falls, but advanced societies provide ever more skills, knowledge and the products of higher and higher technology. There lies in this situation a huge and frightening problem of adjustment of global wage levels. At a conservative estimate the move to market-orientated production in the newly industrializing world is going to increase the global labour force by 1.2 billion during the next generation. The vast majority of these workers at present earn less than three dollars a day – possibly less following the recent currency crisis in Asia. How are their interests to be reconciled with those of 250 million largely North American and European workers who earn 30 times as much? Some commentators foresee wage depression of up to 50 per cent in some areas, and/or unemployment reaching 20 per cent in developed economies.

Governments faced with angry electorates in such circumstances will face appalling choices. These choices are basically about whether to resist or accept the consequences of globalization. Resistance means either forcing down domestic wage levels in order to restore a competitive labour market and bring about the return of jobs, though at much lower rates of pay, or trying to isolate the domestic economy by means of protection. Both will be difficult but in almost reverse ways. The first could not be achieved without serious social consequences and the probable breakdown of the political will to maintain the policies required in the face of massive public objections to the wholesale lowering of living standards. The second, protectionism, carries a strong risk of being unsustainable in a globalized economic environment. The tit-for-tat penalties that protectionism would induce would be economically unpleasant in themselves and ultimately futile, since the global communications system makes isolation of every kind impossible to maintain. This problem becomes highlighted every time there is renewed public discussion of the dilemma all governments find themselves in when trying to determine policies in the national interest. It is ever more difficult to reach consensus about what the national interest actually is. The effects of globalization mean that part of the national economic interest may be bound up in the fate of externally based companies partly operating within national territory. How American or Japanese is an American-manufactured Japanese automobile – a Toyota built in Tennessee – for example? It may equally be that the operations of nationally based companies overseas also represent part of the national economic interest, and that neither of these categories is amenable to any traditional version of what government policy might be. How British is the operation of a British investment house in, say, the Singapore stock market? And how much more difficult to answer when what it has invested in is not located in Singapore at all. 'Who is Us?' becomes an unanswerable question; and questions about ownership of national assets equally imponderable. No doubt versions of these resisting policies will be tried in various locations and it will be possible to judge how effective or ineffective they will turn out to be.

Policies which accept the potential advantages of globalization, on the other hand, will mean not attempting to stem the outward flow of manufacturing industry to cheaper labour markets, but concentrating on the development of ever more highly developed technology and knowledge, both in educational and industrial terms. The intention has to be that the wealth thus generated will create inward-flowing resources sufficient to maintain a deliberately generous reconstructed system of social welfare at the expense of employment. The message of such a response for lifestyle expectations, most specifically the meaning of work, for educational practices and for the fabric of society generally is revolutionary; but it may be a less destructive revolution than that inherent in the probable results of policies of resistance. The immediate dilemma that may arise is well illustrated by the position of the United States as it was in 1999: its economic success, running on a cycle both different and faster from that of the rest of the world, brought with it an almost unimaginably huge trade deficit, particularly with Asia. Dangerous and threatening as this appeared to be, any attempt to deal with it using traditional methods ran the risk of inducing a domestic recession which would in turn render the deficit unsustainable. This would very probably kick-start a global depression from which the United States would be likely to suffer more than others. The price of acceptance is thus a further loss of economic sovereignty – a loss not necessarily easy for electorates and legislatures to understand.

It would be easy in the face of problems such as these, which help to demonstrate that an important part of the role of national governments is to refrain from intervening in the market, to throw the baby out with the bath water and declare their functions to be largely over. This view can be reinforced by remembering that some governments are already – and more need to start – exiting from responsibilities that have either disappeared elsewhere or are better handled in the private sector. However, where this leads to improved efficiency in the functions that remain, the effect is positive and not negative. It is the task of governments to make the global economic system work both better and more acceptably. First and foremost in this is the hard task of arranging socially just reliefs for those economically destroyed by the advance of globalization, thus preserving the basic fabric of society. It is part of the provision of social capital and common goods. Governments may not be the only agencies for achieving this, but in their localities they are the most important. Similarly they are the initiators of policies and regulations promoting environmental protection and health and safety standards. Thereafter, there is a further substantial list of potentially useful, sometimes essential, government activities. They need to improve their information and statistical data-providing services. They need to set the rules governing the economic environment in an effort to restrain the excesses of the market and discourage corruption. They need to be the facilitators of efficient factor and product markets and the guardians of the legal and commercial institutions underpinning these markets, as well as the rules and standards which overarch market transactions. It is also important for governments to oversee the provision of constantly upgraded communications and other physical infrastructures so as to offer the best possible immobile assets to capital that might thus be encouraged to import its mobile assets and so boost employment. Encouraging innovation, particularly among small to medium-sized enterprises, is another highly beneficial activity of a similar kind. Finally, their representative capacity remains significant. Governments have the principal means of protecting national economic interests at international meetings of associations of states, such as the World Trade Organization (WTO) or the IMF, even if their roles are becoming more problematic. Overall, what is lost in terms of economic sovereignty and the ability to pursue macroeconomic policies is balanced by new responsibilities created by the onset of fully global capitalism.

The need for governments is not disappearing, but it is being reconfigured, and as far as populations are concerned the resulting changes can look like serious loss of authority. It is this sense of losing a role which creates the problem of decaying political legitimacy, which will be discussed in section 2.2, and at the same time makes it more difficult for governments to accommodate themselves to their contemporary responsibilities. Setting local rules, relieving distress, doing everything possible to stimulate inward investment, even creating the general moral and political atmosphere in which global capitalism operates locally, important as they are, simply does not look like traditional sovereignty. It is yet another contradiction of globalization that national governments are both losers and gainers; however, the losses have led to political weakness, sufficient to make their remaining and new responsibilities difficult to fulfil.

Global private companies

If the consequences of globalization for markets and for national governments are volatility in the first and deeply puzzling for the second, the same is true for organizations whether commercial or public. A tendency, paralleling that occurring in the experience of national governments, has developed for formerly vertically arranged business structures to be flattened into more horizontal shapes. This has arisen partly out of the need to respond to the global/local paradox that we have already noted. The telecommunications revolution has removed the need for multinational firms to have a single international presence and thus to see each other as ranged against, or at least different from, other firms – almost as if they were commercial versions of states. Nor do they need to support their core activity, whatever it might be, by running a variety of other related activities so as to keep the whole operation 'in house'. Being a globally functioning entity has become even more desirable than being a multinational corporation once was. In the later 1950s, multinational corporations were generally nationally based concerns, having distinctively national characteristics. They operated multinationally, but there was little intra-firm trade or fdi between the subsidiaries. They walked upright in the economic landscape and dealt with each other and national governments from that posture. A change of posture is now very evident: look, for example, at the tendency for formerly national airlines to go global in their cooperative partnerships and to compete by putting emphasis on the global reach which those associations give them. Even their symbols tend to drop the resonance with a national tradition and substitute motifs which are either global in significance or have none at all. The redesign of the tailplanes on British Airways aircraft in the late 1990s is a particularly good illustration of this – the distinctively British national marking gave way to a wide range of colourful but entirely abstract designs, and even a 1999 modification leaves the national motif somewhat vague.

Multinational entities increasingly view the world as a single entity for obtaining supplies, finance and for providing them with markets. The global company has subsumed the multinational both in its style and operationally because of the arrival of fully global markets, the availability of a global labour force, the emergence of global electronic commerce and, with some commodities, the existence of a global culture creating global fashions. These can work both positively and negatively: Coca-Cola is an example of the first, and the late 1990s decline in the fashion for Levis jeans of the second. On the other hand, there is no longer any need for a solidly hierarchical structure of administration, since links are best created horizontally rather than vertically, which tends to flatten out the systems and greatly reduce the size of the central offices of major corporations. Similarly, there is a conjunction between the development of regionalism and the desire of global companies to have manufacture done in the most advantageous place – anywhere in the world. Flexibility of communication and administration now means that it is better to create global coalitions of regionally based firms, whose local existence is socially desirable and politically acceptable and can be the object of locally decided advantages – for example in tax breaks or favourable variations in zoning regulations. Here it is possible to make a marriage between the needs of the global company and the rising significance of regional and local activities, cultural, economic and political. The ability to 'think global and act local' also affects what is produced as well as where and how it is produced. The emergence of a global culture is balanced by a reaction to it, and to global economic and political power, which emphasizes local particularities: of tradition, of taste, of expectation. The flexibilities of the contemporary global firm allow it to produce goods and services that are tailored to local preferences, and gain competitive advantage thereby, while also serving global markets with other products. It is another example of the contemporary economic paradoxes at work. Yet another is that one effect of this has been to create a renaissance of the small to medium-sized firm, in a world that also sees a procession of major global mergers, by which the giant becomes even more dominant in the market for high technology and branded goods and services.

Nor does the process stop here. The emergence of the new-style global firm, with its concentration on core activities has changed the essentially adversarial nature of the previous competition between international companies. One result has been the emergence of inter-firm alliances. The increase has been startlingly brisk, and the intention is to improve penetration of new markets, share costs and speed up the process of innovation. The same feature is to be seen in research and development. At a time of vastly accelerated technological obsolescence, leading to closer interdependence between cutting edge technologies and more immediate effects of research and development on manufacturing processes, both the importance and the costs of the exercise have risen. The result has been hitherto unimaginable cooperation in the field of research and development between firms, despite the fact that their ultimate fate is to be commercial rivals. Of course, these developments pose difficult problems – not least when to cooperate and when to compete, but the contemporary plasticity in these notions is creating a new kind of alliance capitalism in which there is no mutual exclusivity between them but a synergy of competition and cooperation. In this respect the adjustments to new global conditions being made by multinational firms are more sensitive and successful than the more stumbling responses being made by national governments.

A good example of this tendency arises out of the problem of corruption. Some degree of corruption has always been endemic in both government and commerce throughout history. The more economically and politically developed societies became, the more damaging and inconvenient extensive and pervasive corruption appeared to be, and it became a part of the modern state's duty to legislate against it and enforce that legislation. Traditional and deep-seated corruption continued and continues in less developed areas, where, as globalization brings rapid development opportunities, it becomes less and less acceptable and a perceptible hindrance both to a genuine free market and to the rule of law in a Western sense, which itself is a crucial contribution to the context for successful economic development. For the national governments concerned, weakened by other aspects of globalization which we will discuss further in Chapter 3, the reform of corruption has proved too difficult to achieve in any adequate sense. Into the gap have moved multinational companies, who, via their own internal policies and behaviour and by remarkable displays of cooperative solidarity in individual countries, have gone some way towards taking over the functions of the state in this respect and in these places.

Moreover, they have done so in other ways as well. The tendency for governments to collapse where either they have been subject to very great pressures, or where the institutions of the modern state were never deeply rooted in any case, has created administrative crises of a kind so serious that they make economic activity impossible. They also lead to political disruption and bitter conflict which has the same effect except for those who trade in armies and armaments. We shall later see that private organizations of many kinds, rather than other states or their associations are tending to supply the deficiencies in governance that inevitably occur, but it is also worth noting that in some cases, private companies are doing so, too. It is a practice well known in history. Both the Dutch and the British created East India companies which preceded their own direct rule in Indonesia and India respectively, and there were also examples in the Ottoman Empire. But the practice had largely ceased and what was expected was the indirect influence rather than the direct involvement of public companies with foreign governments.

At the end of the twentieth century, it is notable that what is 'foreign', certainly in economic terms, can be quite obscure; and that direct involvement in and assistance to administrative infrastructures by commercial enterprises is now part of the extraordinarily complex weave of the global political economy. Examples of this kind of behaviour are most common in Africa, particularly in the eastern Congo and in the relationship between a whole district of Nigeria and the Chevron Oil Company. A newer and rather different version of the same idea is emerging in discussions in developed countries where it is being suggested that the best interests of companies will be served, when times are hard and specifically when employment moves out of an area, by the introduction of company-run and company-financed schemes of social welfare. It can no longer be assumed that governments can or will undertake the burden of avoiding the social dislocation that unrelieved downsizing will cause, or subsequently control the public disorder that may follow.

Global public entities

As we have seen, markets, national governments and multinational companies have all been profoundly affected by globalization: so, too, have organizations with a global economic function. To put it that way suggests only half the problem that has arisen – the difficulties which beset existing bodies. There is a second half which involves the need for bodies that do not yet exist. Existing economic organizations have their roots in a past international economic environment in which national governments were the primary cooperative actors, and multinational companies were the primary competitive agents. Today, these roles are becoming reversed. In the past, international economic organizations were there to see to it that states and their societies obtained the best deal that benevolent cooperation could impose on private economic competition. This meant that the main organizations, or context-setting decisions like the post-Second World War Bretton Woods agreement on currencies, represented the wishes and actions of states. The International Monetary Fund (IMF), the World Bank, the General Agreement on Trade and Tariffs (GATT) – now the WTO – and the International Labour Organization (ILO) were and are all associations of states. When decolonization produced many new and often

less economically developed states, who felt that the world economic order was stacked against their interests, they developed
organizations to represent that view which were also associations of
states. A feature of the later Cold War period was the emergence of
regional trade blocs – the EEC in Western Europe, ASEAN in South
East Asia, NAFTA in North America and Mercosur in South America,
to name those which to a greater or lesser extent have succeeded in
moving towards regional free trade. These organizations, too, are
associations of states. One of them, the European Union (EU), has
taken the first steps towards creating a semi-state out of a trading
bloc and is unique in the world. A problem arises for them because
of the degree to which their roles have been overtaken by events.
Their progenitors – states – are not beneficiaries of economic globalization, but great global companies have been among the gainers,
and they in any case do not compete in the way they once did. The
contemporary problem that afflicts the World Health Organization
(WHO) is an example. Part at least of its original purpose was to
advance the interests of its member states in health matters and to
restrain the disadvantages that followed from the commercial priorities of the drug companies. Contemporary developments now mean
that world health may best be improved by cooperation between
the WHO acting globally and drug companies, equally acting
globally over both research and development and manufacture.
This means abandoning the basic assumption of an inevitable war
between national governments and drug manufacturers and, in
turn, the idea that the WHO is there to represent the immediate
interests of its members rather than the health of individuals.

The economic structure of the world is simply different; but as
yet, the duties, objectives and proprietors of the main organizations
concerned have not changed. It is not now companies, or even perhaps economic cycles, which require regulation and amelioration so
much as the volatile global markets in stocks, currencies and capital;
and it may not be governments, to whom regulation or advice or
assistance was always applied, who are able to respond to such treatment. The example of the 1998/99 crisis in Indonesia is a case in
point. Here was an economic crisis which was certainly partly
brought on by a notably opaque and corrupt system of government:
the system was neither new nor unique, particularly not in its
region. However, the reason it suffered a crisis and subsequent

political collapse was less its unsatisfactory domestic corruption so much as the activities of currency speculators, who hunt in their own global jungle and who were moving on from a killing in Thailand to a new victim. The institutional response to this was to heap advice and money – provided the advice was at least accepted, if not heeded – on to the Indonesian government. That government was too weak to implement the advice without inducing public disorder, which made the advice inappropriate, and the government was in any case not the only and probably not the principal cause of its own woes, which made the advice – and the money – irrelevant. The element of Greek tragedy in the whole affair came from the fact that the agency whose task was to relieve the crisis, the IMF, could work only according to rules which derived from its origin as an association of states. This both heavily influenced the policy prescriptions it handed out, since they represented the economic convictions of the chief contributing states and compelled it to deal only with the government of Indonesia, which promptly collapsed.

The ongoing and more complex economic collapse in the Russian Federation, together with the hitherto unthinkable quantities of funds which have simply disappeared, either stolen from newly privatized concerns or abstracted from foreign aid, provides further examples of the haphazard irrelevancies which circumstances have forced on the major economic institutions and highlighted the uncomfortable role of the World Bank. It is instructive to learn that the World Bank has acquired a concern with corruption and a sensitivity to moral hazard in the wake of this fiasco. The period 1998/99 saw a perceptible change in the way in which the chief executives of both the World Bank and the IMF spoke about the purposes and responsibilities of their institutions: a striking new awareness of the social and political consequences of their actions was to be observed. It is not surprising that loud voices call for the reforms which would give to these, or other institutions, an independently global role to play; nor is it odd that these voices should be countered by others urging the continued rights and duties of member governments: the contradictions may be awkward, but they are real.

The problems just discussed apply particularly to global public entities which provide resources. There are other types of entity as well. There are those which primarily coordinate action pursued by regional or national institutions. They are generally issue-based: environment, air traffic control, health, for example, and there is some evidence of globally directed strategies emerging. Others are basically information gatherers and holders, parts of the UN and the Organization for Economic Cooperation and Development (OECD) are examples, and they can act as initiators of international discussions, leading to supranational action. Lastly, there are those like the WTO which are essentially rule setters. The role of the WTO has a particularly interesting angle in that its attempts to produce a level playing field in trade can in some circumstances produce an opposite result for some of its members. In environmental policy, raising the costs of environmentally sensitive products may have the effect of discriminating against developing countries vis-à-vis developed countries that willingly embrace high environmental standards. Overall, the brief of the WTO has been extended to include foreign direct investment, intellectual property rights, environment and competition policies as well as cross-border trade in goods and services. Its global remit means that it will have to deal with disputes on these issues between international entities – for example, the EU and the Association of South East Asian Nations (ASEAN) – as well as disputes between states and such bodies, or between state and state.

The most urgent, potentially critical, problem which either a more powerful WTO or any new world economic organization must tackle is that of volatility in the financial markets. As we have already noted, huge sums cross the exchanges every day and are particularly subject to large speculative movements. These are capable of destabilizing the efforts of both the World Bank and the IMF. There are few, if any, accepted 'rules of the game' such as those that regulate global trade in goods and services. Governments have not been successful in introducing schemes controlling capital flows, partly because of the risk of market failure and partly because recipient countries may not be able to absorb such flows. What is needed is an entity which it is agreed will minimize the effects of moral hazard in cross-border investment guarantee schemes; increase transparency in institutional lending and borrowing; ensure that where rescue packages are arranged, those who created the crisis in the first place will at least not benefit from them; be realistic in relation to actual conditions, institutional and systemic, in the countries and regions involved; to persuade governments to be both more effective and more punctual in forestalling economic disasters by improving and strengthening their own regulatory bodies and controlling their domestic financial markets; and to pursue policies designed to narrow if not close the growing gaps, especially among developing countries, which are so obviously opening up in the global economy.

Effective management of a global economy in the interests of its increasingly numerous and vocal participants can only be derived from a balanced mixture of subnational, national and global representation in fully global organizations. The creation of such a hybrid will be the task of the next century: for the moment, we have an irreversibly global economic context, but our troubles, failures and frightening anxieties chiefly arise from the absence of any machinery for managing it. If it evolves, the benefits of globalization will predominate; if it does not, the inherent risk of economic and political chaos, followed by increasingly widespread violence will become reality. In any such reforms there will continue to be a significant, if lesser, role for national governments to play, not least as guardians of local economic rules and transparent and uncorrupt domestic administration, and, even more seriously, to seek out ways of engaging with the new sources of economic power and influence which globalization has created. This is a hard proposition, because the global markets are only just beginning to see that their own effectiveness and convenience can only be secured if they generate their own cooperative systems of regulation, possessing legitimate authority, in order to combat their chaotic volatility. When that happens a kind of role reversal will have taken place. National governments, who used to be the source of cooperation, have already become serious competitors at many levels for the inward investment that globalization has made available, while companies and the global markets in which they operate, who used to compete, have become the readier source of much effective cooperation. There are tentative signs of this development in the global stock market, in global banking and in the management of the Internet, none as yet in the currency markets. It is an important empty space, and it will be a space to watch.

2.2   Governance and peoples

Introduction

In section 2.1 we have seen the transformation of the machinery of global communications as well as that of the global economic and financial system, and we have seen some of the contradictory pressures that these evolutions are generating. In the main, although these pressures are expressed in very differing modes, they arise from a common tension. The tension is between the general – or global – and the particular – or local. Put another way, it is between the de-territorialized organization and the precisely located individual. What makes it possible for both to exist within one social environment is the sleepless and placeless global communications system. What in turn, makes this into a tension rather than just a fact is that it erodes the available means human society has so far developed for resolving tensions between the needs of the whole and the freedom of the individual, while supplying – thus far at least – no alternative. This is a rather formal way of describing what is actually happening to nation states and their governments.

The state and the various forms of government that it has evolved over time have been the mechanism by which most human societies – not all – have resolved, as far they have been able to, the essential contradiction between achieving the best conditions of life for the majority and what each person might want for themselves. The most acceptable routes for arriving at the compromises which thus have to be made have been tested and retested, written down as constitutions and precedents and enshrined in law. The shorter-term adjustments and modifications which are always required are the stuff of daily political life and inform the ideologies of regimes, sometimes leading to tough dictatorships, more frequently to brands of democracies. Resistance movements in the first case and the urgent vigour of political parties in the second have been the chosen engines for propelling that political life. Whatever its individual style, the state and the particular government it has extruded at any given moment have been the place where the great political choices on economic and social issues have been made. It possessed the kind of power which makes the governing of societies possible because of a public acceptance that such government is both necessary and effective. It confers political legitimacy and thus political authority. If either of those conditions is weakened or disappears, confusion results and familiar distributions of power come into question and may be operationally challenged in ways that stretch between mild unrest and violent, revolutionary, change. It is therefore not surprising that these structures loom so large and it is no more surprising that there is a contemporary tendency to ask increasingly worried questions about their health and effectiveness.

One reason for this anxiety is that the state has occupied this central position for a very long time and it is not easy for people to think that it was ever different and thus might as easily be different again. It is not an area in which change is easy to contemplate. However, looked at with a late-twentieth-century eye, it is clearly becoming easier to see that states have not only been creatures of a particular period but that even during their primacy of people's political imaginations, other groupings of authority or activity – polities – have existed concurrently. The apparently dominant role of the state has always been more apparent than real. The force of the idea, nonetheless, is not to be underestimated, even if the process of demythologizing it may turn out to be easier than might have been predicted. Thus it is important to understand that the state was the product of a particular place and time in human development which took root deeply and naturally in many parts of the world, and was imposed and operated more shallowly elsewhere, until by the end of the nineteenth century it had ceased to be possible for people to imagine an alternative: it might be differently represented, it might be the object of revolutionary attempts to change its immediate political character, but the institution itself had become a given condition – so much so that one of the last great efforts to generalize its functions in a particular way, as proposed by Karl Marx, thought of itself as supplanting and abolishing all other forms.

The cause of anxiety about the contemporary role of the state lies in the complex and often contradictory results of the global communications revolution which we have been discussing. To recapitulate therefore: the conjunction of microchip computers and the orbiting satellite has brought in its wake a fundamental restructuring of the global economy. The effect has been to abolish state frontiers as far as the traffic of information, particularly technological knowledge, is concerned. This has created a global market in technologically dependent commodities. At the same time, ease of communication and thus control and command has made it possible for globally operating businesses to locate their activities wherever local conditions make it most desirable to do so. This has brought basic manufacturing work to formerly underdeveloped economies and subtracted it from advanced ones. One paradoxical result of this has stemmed from a marked increase in global migration flows, partly made possible by the ease of contemporary travel. But two motives chiefly fuel it: one is the wish to escape from cruel political or economic conditions and the other is to go in pursuit of better-paid work or better state welfare systems. The result in a country like Germany is that migrants may arrive seeking better paid work in a society where unemployment is high and rising because manufacturing has itself migrated to where wages are lower. When the persistent economic boom of the late 1990s in the United States slows down, the same effect will be seen there. The problems associated with migration are severe, ranging from housing to health and crime. Governments are not proving capable of controlling it, and have not or are politically unable to deliver the resources to deal effectively with its awkward domestic consequences.

Before looking more closely at the problems surrounding the future of the state, we should also quickly revisit the economic context. The activities of deeply integrated multinational enterprises, together with the cross-border inter-firm alliances that they engender, have become the principal form of international transactions. Banking and stock market activity has gone in the same direction and has little or no geographical location left: it exists where there are terrestrial monitors connected to cyberspace. The picture that emerges is of a global economic system of great complexity. Significant participants in the preceding interdependent global economy, governments, groups of governments, territorially based markets and banks, and multinational companies dealt with each other as singular, temporally and physically located entities. They thus acted in ways that were analogous with, if not sharing their mechanisms, the kind of essentially vertical relationship which states had established with each other since the seventeenth century. These vertical relationships remain in the new situation, but their roles are different and generally reduced, and their physical shapes, formerly pyramidal, have tended to flatten and spread. Global markets, global manufacturers and purveyors of knowledge, and global consumers, already either horizontal in shape or lacking any physical shape at all, have arrived as new participants, stirring like a rising mist on a summer's morning round the soaring trunks of the trees in an old wood. They move inexorably across global space and time without respect to physical geography, political frontiers, or night and day.

These economic effects have been joined by others. News, comment and information of all kinds have taken on an independent life of their own, divorced from the control of governments. Defence and the conduct of war have been affected similarly and occupy a transitional position in which national defence mechanisms and attitudes survive, but often have to be expressed through cooperative peacemaking or peacekeeping operations. All this vigorous life, intellectual, technological and commercial, is being conducted horizontally, cutting across the old vertical divisions typical of the traditional state. What are the consequences for the state? Can it be remoulded to fit contemporary requirements? If so, it can only be by reducing expectations as to what functions it can best perform and fitting it into a much more pluralistic global system of governance.

This will be very hard. The weight of tradition is against it and the traditional state can come to be seen as a defence against those aspects of economic globalization which are not popular. On the other hand, what it needs to do for the benefit of its people in the global economy can only be tough and unpopular. Meanwhile, some of its authority trickles away in the face of the instinctive as well as practical realization on the part of electorates that many of its functions have been eroded by global change. Thus a paradox remains for resolution: there is a job for the state to do, but it is hard to do, and the same events that have produced that job have also reduced the political legitimacy of the state to the point where public support for tough measures is much less easy to assemble and maintain. And if the state tries to resist globalization, it will be equally if not more difficult and require privations on the part of the people, which they may not be willing to accept from a weakened system of government. The best outcome will be uncomfortable evolutionary change, the worst, of which there are already clear warnings, will be public disorder leading to the collapse of the existing institutions of government and the probability of more general disturbances.

There is another side to this coin which complicates the problem further. Because the exercise of public domestic authority came to be associated almost completely with states, the devices which have been developed to make that authority acceptable to populations have also been linked to the machinery of states. These devices consist of constitutional limitations and other conditions that are imposed on the exercise of power. They are part of the expected, necessary, structure of the national state and it is their governments and rulers who have, willingly or unwillingly, to accept them. Democratic systems of government provide further means of mediating power. Both constitutional limitations and democratic systems, when in full working order, supply political legitimacy and therefore public consent for the exercise of power. When power and authority begin to seep away from national governments, they also escape from the controls which have evolved in association with states, and from their democratic systems, wherever they exist. Newer sources of globalized power and authority are being exercised without any of the familiar and expected restraints, thus destroying the link between public acceptance that power must be exercised and the maintenance of some controls over it. This produces in global circumstances what in the regional conditions of the EU has been described as a democratic deficit. In that case the exercise of power, subtracted from member states by administrative organs in Brussels, has not yet been subjected to the ultimate control of the European Parliament, and the actions of individual European Commissioners have only very recently been the object of its scrutiny. Pressure for greater accountability is mounting and some changes are evolving, but, like the Parliament's defective control over the European budget, there is a long road to walk yet.

In global terms, the road has not even been mapped out, let alone constructed. The vast powers of employment or unemployment, the ability to confer riches or poverty, the provision of knowledge and immediate information, all of which now lie so markedly with global operating areas of power, are bereft of public participation, still less control. There is no machinery for achieving this and a dearth of ideas about how to do so. Put bluntly: who ever elected a currency speculator? Or, perhaps even more sinisterly, how can there be any democratic influence over the World Wide Web Consortium (W3C) who exercise great power both administrative and potentially political – through censorship – over the Internet? Or, similarly, how can the public have any say over the effort by the Global Business Dialogue to make sure that it is the business users who control electronic commerce and prevent it from coming under any management by governments? Given the obvious significance of electronic commerce both for the potential defrauding or indebting of individuals, in addition to its use as an instrument of transnational crime, the political implications are serious. What public participation is there in the appointment of the President of the World Bank? The latter figure, interestingly, turned up in 1999 at the funeral of the late King Hussein of Jordan in the company of and listed with actual heads of state, including the President of the United States of America.

All these examples raise the issue of the vertical, wherein lies existing legitimacy, and the horizontal, wherein lies power, in an acute form. For there is a direct clash of interest between the evolution of horizontal limitations on the exercise of horizontal power and the vertically arranged structures and controls with which we are familiar, if increasingly disenchanted. In the past, an acceptable exercise of power was achieved through violence as much or more than by evolutionary change, and the fact is at least a warning if not a prediction. There is an urgent and growing need, therefore, to begin developing new systems, global in scope, in order to reproduce the controlling effects on horizontally exercised power which were long ago developed within states to restrain the abuse of vertically exercised authority. These will not necessarily be echoes of those devised in the light of the evolution of the state. It is more likely that the shape of successful alternative validations of global sources of power will turn out to be very different if they are to guard against violent rejections of irreversibly established global authorities when people discover how uncontrolled they actually are. This problem amounts to a contemporary crisis of governance and political legitimacy. It requires that the traditional means of protecting citizens from over-mighty rulership be reduced and redirected, while at the same time allowing globally focused controls to evolve, shaped to match the sources of power they are intended to restrain. The vertical and the horizontal have to be accommodated within a single system. This is clearly such a serious matter that it will be worth taking a much closer look at it. The fundamental problem – making the existence and exercise of power acceptable to individuals – has not changed, but its practical expression has; and as human society has at least one highly significant historical experience of solving it, it would not be sensible to think about the contemporary situation without knowing something about how the existing arrangements came about.

The governance of states

The most complex forms of political relationship and commercial and cultural exchange have developed over the last 300 years and have been the product of an era when most societies turned themselves into or aspired to become nation states. Such evolutionary changes usually produced episodes of conflict and warfare. The study of these relationships and particularly their occasional descent into violence, has become an intellectual discipline, rising to greater and greater sophistication as it has sought to understand more about the shifting sands of inter-state activities, economic, political and strategic. It is useful to remember this pattern because it lasted for so long that it came to be regarded as a given condition, an unchanging basis for discussion, an inalienable template by which to explain the affairs of states and their external relations. This in turn helps to throw light on why much muddle and anxiety have developed in the face of recent fundamental evolutionary shifts which have invalidated the template: these are the shifts in both power and the distribution of power which have come to be called globalization, and we shall look longer at their international effects in Chapter 3.

In order to assess further the contemporary internal impacts of globalization, we need to discuss the consequences of the successive technological revolutions in communications described in section 2.1. Their influence on both internal political stability and external relationships since the early nineteenth century has been profound. Both the machinery of international relations and the fixed assumptions which societies have come to make about the likely consequences of their own or their government's actions have been shaped by the effects which technological change has had on the nature and distribution of power – economic and political. On the whole, the period from the middle of the nineteenth century to the later part of the twentieth can be seen as a single evolution, itself emerging from an earlier and more geographically restricted version of a similar structure. In both these situations, as we shall see, the principal propelling agent in the equations of power was the unfolding development of the state, both internally and externally. After about 300 years of continuous, expansionary, activity, it is not surprising that the central role of the state itself, never mind what whirligigs of changing fortune might occur between them, became a fixed expectation, a given condition of the political life of humanity. Nor is it surprising that the world steadily acquired the mechanisms that matched the realities on the ground.

Understanding how and why this situation developed is an essential precondition for appreciating why the contemporary environment can seem so alarmingly strange, where familiar, previously reliable, points of reference no longer provide baselines, as if the lighthouses that make sense of difficult coasts had been switched off. The contemporary world is seeing change on a greater scale and at a deeper level than anything that has happened since the sovereign state began to evolve in Europe towards the end of the sixteenth century: the lighthouses really have been turned out and it is crucial to comprehend where the coastline really is if we are to make sense of the inevitable, and potentially violent, transitions which must occur.

The overwhelming difficulties of land transport before the machine age affected almost every aspect of human life. Internally it meant that all forms of centralized government were bound to be weak at best or merely amoebic at worst and that it was highly localized units which most affected everyday life, even if they were formally part of and subject to a loosely structured larger entity. The difficulty also affected external relationships. During the Roman Empire, for example, ordinary diplomatic exchanges were rendered almost impossible by the length of time it might take for an embassy to find the Emperor, whose court – and therefore the government – had a strong tendency to be peripatetic. In such an immense space it was easy to miss and difficult to catch up with the constantly moving target that the Imperial entourage represented. In general circumstances like these, the advantages lay with seaborne traffic, for commerce, information and strategy. Coasts tended to enjoy higher civilization and greater wealth, but also to be a focus for conflict. Political entities which enjoyed effective water communication tended to be more sophisticated administratively, and any technological improvement in ships extended their commercial and naval reach. By the sixteenth century the Chinese had already visited East Africa, though they did not follow up on their seagoing expertise, and in Europe, the Portuguese, the Venetians, the Genoese, the Spanish, the English and the Dutch were demonstrating the importance of water-borne communications and naval power. Those who did not have such access were either restrained – for example the Russians locked into the Eurasian land mass behind ice-bound ports – or showed signs of failing development, as the largely landlocked Holy Roman Empire did in Germany and Central Europe.

At much the same time, other factors, particularly the consequences of the emergence of fully monetarized economies and the secularizing effects of the Reformation, caused the gradual evolution of fully independent states in Europe. The decline of formerly pan-European, Roman originated, forms of authority, both religious and political, allowed individual rulers to assert their own untrammelled legal and political jurisdiction which they were able to establish over the rights of local lords within their territories as well as excluding former external suzerains. The result was a downsizing of the most effective political unit; and the further result was that entities emerged which were small enough to be able to ignore the serious problems of communication over long distances. The improved possibilities for their internal administration which followed further reinforced the authority of sovereign or nearly sovereign rulers.

The consequence was a maelstrom of internal and external conflict in Europe, lasting for a century. The movement of power flowed away from highly traditional authorities, to some degree still legitimized by the Roman inheritance and away from highly localized barons and princes whose position was based upon ancient rights by which they could command services and goods in kind. Authority now flowed towards the rulers of states who based their claim to internal and external sovereignty on their ability to provide coherent and functional administration, essentially paid for out of monetary wealth obtained from taxation, borrowing or seizure. These new-style regimes were providing a stability regarded by populations as necessary in an age when their numbers were rising, recovering after the trauma of the Black Death, and at a time of quickening economic and commercial activity. But they were also the benefi- ciary of another development. Changes in the nature of power did not just affect new users. The fact that there were new users also meant that there were consequential changes in the distribution of power, away from the centres of the past, which created one kind of conflict and into new hands, among whom the pecking order was as yet uncertain, which created another. The wars which wracked Europe from the beginning of the sixteenth century were the conse- quence. Their climax came in the period 1618–48, but they did not finally abate until 1713. They began as struggles to defend or reject the older dispensations, religious wars and wars surrounding the position of the Holy Roman Empire and its Habsburg rulers. After 1648, the new had essentially triumphed over the old and turned to the business of settling a new distribution of power among the beneficiaries. This chiefly turned on the question of whether the French, who came to full statehood first among European societies, would be able to transform their advantage into a European hege- mony. The answer was that they could not, and that answer was to have powerful effects on contemporary international politics. An additional effect of so much conflict over so long a period was to create a basis of loyalty within societies whose citizens had suffered so much together. They came to see themselves as ranged together against others, as communities, political and economic, as well as units of sovereign government.

In one sense this smoothed the path of the sovereign ruler. In another, it created intense problems. The supplanting of loose, tradi- tional forms of authority may have been supported by secularization and by the need for unity in the face of external conflict, but these alone did not supply legitimacy and thus a secure and well-based regime. There had been substantial restrictions on the practical operation of traditional political and legal controls. The source was likely to be distant, and where it was local there were obvious practi- cal reasons why local lords would be more effectively served by dri- ving on a comfortable rein rather than using the whip. Their presence was highly personal and their reward was goods and ser- vices. The contrast with the incoming system was important. The domestic power of sovereign rulers was significantly greater and their rule more tightly organized, if nowhere near the expectation that a late-twentieth-century citizen might have. Societies, understandably, turned out to want a substitute for the natural restrictions on the use and abuse of power that would be effective in the new situation; and they particularly wanted it in respect of taxation. At different paces and in different places, the combination of the arguments of political philosophers and the often violent objections of populations, began to force an entirely new set of restrictions on the power of rulers. The growing authority of the English Parliament, followed by the military defence of its role within the English system of government, including as it did the execution of the King, is the classic example of a process where the acquisition of great power was quickly followed by the evolution of important restraints upon the use of that power. Failure to observe those restraints led to the withdrawal of the consent of the governed and the collapse of political legitimacy. Gradually a vastly complicated rule book of acceptable ways of achieving a stable political society developed, malleable but essential in all advanced states. Maintaining this balance between wielding effective power and preserving the rights of citizens has been part of the evolution of states and we shall have to revisit some of its more modern manifestations in the next subsection.

For now, we need to return to the relationship between communications and the distribution of power which was touched in the introduction to this section. As the significance of central government rose, a balance developed between size, which might yield demographic, resource and strategic advantages, and governability in a practical sense, which could determine how much use could be made of such advantages. Put another way, something like an optimum size for a state emerged, in which it was not so large that communication with its peripheries became too slow for central government to be effective; but, equally, that it was not much smaller, since that reduced the possible advantages to be derived from population and natural resources. Exactly how this balance would work depended on two significant factors: first, how rapid contemporary communications systems actually were. Until the nineteenth century this meant horse relays over land, which were faster or slower according to road quality and weather conditions, and sailing ships by water, which improving techniques from time to time somewhat accelerated. Secondly, it depended upon the relative position which good government occupied among those factors which conferred power. Good, competent, government has not always been as highly valued as it is now or began to be during the seventeenth century. In the early stages of state formation, for example, it was less significant than when rulers had gone further along the road of unification and concentration of territory. Indeed, it was not until the later seventeenth century that defining precise territorial frontiers became as significant as obtaining or maintaining jurisdictional rights, and when this happened maps appeared in treaties and markers appeared on the ground. It was an indication that the responsibilities of government were becoming more defined and that knowing precisely who was a subject had become important: to whom duties were owed and from whom tax revenue might be raised were significant items of information. As the importance of efficient government relatively rose, so did the significance of faster communications techniques.

The process of dividing Europe into independent states was both lengthy and patchy. It was not merely a change of gear, it was a change of engine. It yielded a growing number of entities ranged along a wide spectrum of physical size, population density, resource base and competent rulership. The stresses and strains of installing new systems of government produced much internal conflict and the confusion surrounding the projection of external power resulted in constant warfare. By the end of the seventeenth century, however, the dust began to settle, and a fresh outline became visible. There was a design of a kind for domestic government and it was provided by France. The bones of a modern state administration first appeared in France under the rule of cardinals Richelieu and Mazarin, in the first half of the seventeenth century, and the outburst of international power and domestic civilization which marked the reign of Louis XIV made France the model for Europe in the second half. The relationship between centralized, relatively efficient, administration and the skilful use of intrinsic resources was emphasized by the primacy that France was for a time able to establish, and further suggested that France approximated to the contemporary optimum size for a state. Certainly, if, as has been suggested, a communications time of five days with the peripheries was the limit of effectiveness, then France was just about right.

One of the reasons why France moved on more successfully than some other states was because she achieved an earlier and faster development and was able to use the evident advantages of having done so, to install a monarchical dictatorship – *l'état, c'est moi* – as Louis XIV so famously remarked. This deferred the issue of accommodating the political and legal rights of the population, which, for example, in England led to a Civil War in the middle of the century, until the end of the eighteenth century when it exploded with all the force of a dam bursting. The advance of France was not, however, sufficient to overlay or postpone the development of other states. She was persistently opposed by Spain, who was coming to the end of what could be achieved on the back of imported wealth from Central and South America – wealth that had temporarily given her a special position in the late sixteenth century and permanently affected her view of her proper place in the world. The Dutch, the Habsburgs, a coalition of German states and particularly the English resisted a French hegemony in Europe and ultimately, after the Duke of Marlborough's victories in the War of the Spanish Succession in the 1690s, they were successful; and their success was registered by the Treaty of Utrecht of 1713.

The wars of the first part of the eighteenth century demonstrated the results of having restrained the French but not yet having recognized any stable distribution of power among the other greater states. In fact stabilization was beginning to occur. The effects of the contemporary optimum size, backed by some technical improvement in road building, combined with the benefits of improving administration and political stability, was beginning to make distinctions between European states. States that were either too small, like Venice, Genoa, Portugal, the Netherlands and Sweden, or were inefficient, like Spain, relatively declined. States that were roughly the right size for the period, or could offer efficiency and stability or both, relatively rose. By mid-century, the latter came to include Britain, France, Prussia, Austria (the Holy Roman Empire still in name) and Russia. Each state demonstrated a diverse equation of power. For Russia, there were relative disadvantages arising from her enormous size and unwieldiness. For Britain, there was little if any local benefit to be obtained in the region from her extensive overseas possessions. Had these two factors not been so, there would have been a bipolar system in Europe based on the predominance of

Britain and Russia; but, in practice, the face they presented to the European international system made them more or less the equals of the other powers. The French were unable to recapture former glories because they had stagnated administratively and were eunuchs in terms of any popular basis for political legitimacy. This left them much on a level with the others. The two principal Germanic states and Russia were all the object of serious governmental reform based on the prescriptions of the Enlightenment, which itself derived from the later seventeenth-century experiences of France. The result was a flow of political and administrative activity internally and stalemate externally.

The stalemate expressed itself in warfare and highly active diplomacy which produced little and eventually no results in terms of territorial change in Europe: no one could win, and while bellicosity remained, a practical reluctance actually to go to war set in after the end of the Seven Years War in 1763. The effect of an apparent impossibility of winning was buttressed by another pressure. The more that competent government, or at least competent in contemporary terms, was both required by peoples and necessary as part of the terms of power, the less attractive warfare seemed. The greater concentration of power within states meant that warfare had become a more substantial, expensive and potentially physically damaging activity. The War of the Spanish Succession had been an example, as had the Seven Years War (1756–63). There were thus contradictory pressures emerging: states were highly suspicious of each other because of the even distribution of power, and wished to be able to defend themselves and advance their interests. But rulers were equally conscious that going to war had destructive effects on the domestic sinews of power and compromised the effort to reform and improve domestic management. Moreover, in an age which was apt to produce rationalist rather than religious arguments, the divine right of rulers had ceased to have the force it once did, and even inheritance seemed less compelling than competence. The notion that rulers might rule for as long as they patently attempted to do so in the interests of their populations was likely to put a premium on avoiding war and to increase the level of stress that would be required before rulers would resort to it. Thus, achieving a delicate balance, in an era of more sophisticated state structures, between the demands of the business of government and maintaining security within an international community, became a primary ambition for rulers and their ministers.

Both the internal balance with its resulting political legitimacy and the external balance of power were destroyed by the French Revolution of 1789. Like the English Revolution in the 1640s, it was induced by a breakdown of government in the face of the need to deal with bankruptcy. The right to tax on the part of governments and the right to have an influence on the incidence of taxation and the purposes for which the resulting revenue was spent, had long been an important issue. Quite recently it had figured among the causes of the American War of Independence and had there led to a new statement of the rights of individuals and the duties of government which reflected both English traditions from the preceding century and the writings of contemporary Enlightenment political philosophers. The result was a new mechanism for expressing the relationship between the individual and governments in a constitutionally defined system.

The French Revolution pushed this process further and seriously shifted the previous balance in the direction of more popular participation in the processes of government. This had the effect of increasing a people's perception of itself as a nation in the modern sense. The idea of nationalism, however, also had an important origin in the opposition that eventually developed to Napoleonic hegemony. The Napoleonic Empire was a remarkable combination of old and new. It claimed to be able to realize the best principles of the revolution in terms of good and modern government and to be able to protect and advance the achievements of civilization. It also sought to return to an older, and to some degree imaginary, Europe, which retained its status as a *maxima civitas*, inherited from the days of Rome. In such a Europe, the quarrels and wars of independent states would not occur, peace would be assured and all the benefits of a unitary rule would accrue. To make the point, Napoleon himself occasionally dressed up as a Roman Emperor and sometimes as Charlemagne, while abolishing the Holy Roman Empire but carefully marrying the daughter of the last Emperor. This attempt to reverse the tide of history and suppress a developed community of sovereign states was predictably unsuccessful; and by the end the process of defeating it had induced not only the natural hostility of other rulers but also the opposition of ordinary people who came to see the Napoleonic Imperium as an affront to their nationalities. They thus became amenable to appeals to nationalism as a ground for supporting the war against the Emperor. Once that genie was out of the bottle, it could not be returned and corked up again. The state, which had pre-existed the revolution, as the normal form of organization for European societies, acquired a new object of existence: to represent the well-being and aspirations of a particular ethnic group, or, at least, to contain and be supported by a population of which a majority came from one nationality. This new ingredient in the mix of factors which conferred domestic political legitimacy shifted the distribution of power during the next century. Those states to whom history had given a mixed population, and were thus states without nations, began to decline, and those nationalities which were not represented by a state of their own and were thus nations without states, began to demand that they should acquire statehood and in some cases to achieve that ambition. The Habsburg Empire and the Ottoman Empires belonged to the first category, Italy (1860), Hungary (1867) and Germany (1871) belonged to the second. These three all emerged at the expense of the Habsburg Empire and in the latter case, France as well.

The predominance of the idea of the state itself was increased by these developments: the arguments were all about defending existing states or becoming new states. While this evolution proceeded, other factors were rapidly accelerating the domestic power of governments and thus the political significance of governing. These factors were the consequence of technological advances flowing from the Industrial Revolution and they were to push the nation state into becoming the collectivist state. In virtually every aspect of human existence, more advanced mechanisms, industrially produced, could improve the quality of life. Health, safety, travel, the availability of goods and services were all examples. What was possible was increasingly and comprehensibly demanded by populations. The result was a huge expansion of activity. New forms of construction, for example, for railway lines, new forms of physical plant, like sewage treatment plants, electricity and gas generating facilities, and their vast delivery networks, either fell directly into the scope of government or provoked the establishment of regulatory systems. The result was an unprecedented expansion in the scope and size of the machinery of government – an administrative revolution.

The effect rapidly became circular: new roles required new monies, new monies required new taxation, both required additional state employees whose salaries required further new monies. Thus taxation also inevitably grew and the significance of the machinery of the state in the daily lives of ordinary people became more compelling.

The spread of literacy across far wider sections of populations which followed from improved educational systems created a basis for the growth of a popular press which, anxious to increase its readership and profits, did not hesitate to cast political and even social life in highly dramatic, and often deeply inaccurate, terms. Moreover, governments, finding it ever harder to obtain and then to keep the support of fickle electorates, jumped on to the bandwagon and began to resort to simplified sloganeering internally and to describe foreign policy either in the rhetoric of aggressive nationalism or by emitting loud cries of foul play and a consequent need to defend the fatherland. The awkwardnesses of this situation led to the emergence of two alternative, though in many ways similar, modes of political justification for an intensively active role for government in industrialized societies: communism and fascism. After the catastrophe of the First World War, which itself put the organs of states under intense pressure and greatly expanded their authority, both joined the more traditional liberal, if increasingly collectivist, state not just as theoretical models, but as practical examples. Both, notwithstanding the Marxist belief in the eventual withering away of the state, in practice greatly contributed to the sense of vertical division between them. This division now not only took political, economic and ethnic forms, but ideological as well.

The ideological consequences have worked or are working themselves out in the late twentieth century. The physical and architectural consequences are very much still to be seen. It is somehow easier to comprehend the full weight of the state and its governmental system when we remember to look at its physical expressions as just that, rather than the familiar architectural clothing of capital cities and regional centres. It is not surprising that there was a temporal connection between the opening of the greatest period of state authority and the rebuilding of capital cities. The habit started in the eighteenth century with St Petersburg, followed by Washington. Both sought to give an air of permanence to a state which was in fact under construction. Older state forms had almost accidentally acquired administrative or royal court centres located usually in places already important for strategic or commercial reasons. Until the second half of the nineteenth century, however, they remained jumbled and chaotic masses: a mix of official buildings and palaces and slums.

The needs of an expanding central government machine together with the feelings of an emotionally nationalist society evoked major rebuilding schemes: vast administrative departmental buildings appeared, specifically devoted to named government activities arranged on great avenues, themselves laid out to accommodate the processions by which the national state and/or empire gave expression to their grandeur and individuality. Just how far contemporary activities and needs have changed may be judged from the fact that in the late twentieth century, the Treasury building of the British government, grandly located in Whitehall, the traditional seat of government, was deemed inappropriate for duties which have become principally computerized and can be substantially contracted out. It was made available for conversion, most probably as a hotel. This is, of course, an extreme example. But, particularly in developed countries, the property markets have been and are full of former state civil and military buildings and complexes for sale, not necessarily or even usually very grand, but indicative of a slimming diet in national government machines.

It is equally instructive to observe the contemporary tendency to regard great national cities as museums in themselves and to treat them as such. In the past, they were assumed to be the proper place to locate the great national collections of art and artefacts, themselves often the result of past competitive theft from the place of origin; and sometimes now the object of demands, increasingly successful, for their return. The converse also exists. There has developed a perceptible global similarity in the construction of extremely grand international airports and in their appearance and management. A sleepy traveller might have considerable initial difficulty in deciding where he or she had actually landed; and, if the final destination was a commercial or industrial concern, an equal problem in identifying exactly in which country or continent the building or plant was located. Little in the furniture or general design culture, nothing in the computerized systems and probably not a lot in the language in use would be very helpful, and even climatic difference would be controlled into the background. Of course many places remain where that is not true, but there is no doubt of the tendency or of how far it has already gone.

The swansong of the system of national states came after 1945. The superpowers were to be the last of their kind, stately dinosaurs accompanied by their families awaiting the onslaught of the impacting meteorite. In this case, the analogy with an impact catastrophe will not hold. What was coming had been more like a lesion in the earth's crust, invisible at first, then the source of visible cracks and finally quite suddenly the cause of collapse. As we now know, the agent of this change was the most recent stage in the global communications revolution which had been brewing since the invention of the railway and the electric telegraph. These had remained within the control or, if privately owned, the regulation of states and had enhanced their authority, as well as their potential size. The addition of the oceanic cables in the very early twentieth century globalized international relations in ways which at first emphasized the individual sovereignty of states as well as by increasing the potential geographical scope of their activities. The arrival of the telephone had more of a cementing effect within individual societies and only a limited role in inter-state communications until the later twentieth century. The most recent stage has, however, brought a genuine revolution with it. The combination of the microchip computer and the orbiting satellite has created not so much an improved means for states and societies to communicate with each other, though of course it does that, but a network of communications which exists in its own global environment. The effects have become famous, even notorious, and they have begun to reverse the persistent rise in the role of states and rulers which has been so marked since the seventeenth century.

The result has begun to reverse some if not all of the effects of the verticalization which the creation of states had involved. Human activities are in a sense reverting to horizontal patterns, identifiable by topic rather than geography, by subject rather than ethnicity, but this time they are fully global in their scope and they portend a major reorganization of the way in which human beings order their daily lives. These developments are having noticeable effects in two main areas: on the internal government of states because of the erosion of political legitimacy and because of structural changes required in the machinery of government; on the external relations between states, because they are no longer the sole players on the global stage and, by extension, on inter-state entities, because of the weakened position of their sponsoring bodies and because they, too, have to live in a more pluralistic world.

Political legitimacy

We will discuss first the contemporary problems associated with the idea of political legitimacy, which was discussed at the beginning of this section. The problem starts with the economic changes we noted in the last presentation: manufacturing and commercial activity which was formerly confined to Western Europe, America and Japan can now take place anywhere and is doing so in Asia, Central Europe and China; the result is the emergence of new sources of market outlets and of competition; a growing convergence of living standards among advanced countries and a better appreciation in both developing and developed countries of the part which international business activities can play in improving national competitiveness. These changes have necessarily complex factors underlying them: wealth-creating assets, chiefly people, money and knowledge move freely across national boundaries; natural resources have declined in relative significance while physical capital and human knowledge have increased. The kind of products now being produced require new forms of economic organization, notably cooperative networks and ventures between firms. Competition between governments for global resources and markets has grown and they have to take account of and try to improve the way in which their domestic resources are performing relative to those of other countries so as to benefit the performance of nationally based firms. This is because globalization has produced serious competitive pressure on productivity levels which have to be constantly improved or governments will find domestic living standards falling as economic activity takes itself to more advantageous sites elsewhere.

All of these factors imply that the role of government is changing in two major directions. First, the opportunity of delivering social benefits to their populations, formerly an internal decision, is now crucially dependent on achieving an effective macroeconomic global strategy operating in a horizontal relationship with other entities whether countries, organizations or firms. If such a strategy is either misconceived or mishandled and thus fails in its cooperative aspect, the domestic results are likely to be harrowing. In these circumstances, decisions become much more difficult to arrive at because decision makers have a both internal and external constituency to satisfy, but will probably have to describe their activities in the largely internal terms that electorates can easily comprehend. Secondly, achieving this requires not just changing attitudes but changing the functions of government itself, as firms have already done. Increasingly, the functions required to maximize the investment advantages and jobs to be harvested from the global economy are becoming interdependent and administratively interwoven, yet the actual structures have been slow to follow suit. The old physical administrative extrusions of the sovereign state arranged in vertical boxes of responsibilities cannot cope with a world where competition policy, environment policy, tax policy, innovation policy and education policy must be managed as a coherent whole, undivided by the vested interests of administrative systems located in clearly labelled ministries or departments of state.

Decisions about environmental issues are a good example of the problem. The level at which an environmental question needs to be decided can vary very sharply. It may be very local, but, equally, as in the case of arguments over the disposal of toxic waste, it may be both local, emotionally powerful, and yet external because the point of departure or destination of the waste can easily be far away. It may arise from government action, or inaction, or from private action or inaction. It refuses to be boxed even at that level. It may, however, involve decisions which affect or threaten global climatic change, in which case there is likely to be a muddled combination of national economic interests, private and/or public, the particular interests of other countries or regions and the need to protect the global climatic system as a whole. In this kind of situation, an internal decision made by allowing the trading-off of interests negotiated by government departments between themselves as if they were playing on a level field, is unlikely to lead to an acceptable outcome; still less will it do so when the matter is at the least international but most probably global in scope. To make matters more complex still, environmental issues are an area where the Internet has created a highly vocal and effective global constituency. The pressure comes not so much from organized national groups, or from business interests, against whom it is often directed, but from individuals. The most obvious example of this kind of pressure can be found in the USA and seen at the Internet web site Scorecard. It contains large quantities of accurate information about industrial pollution and polluters which can be directly accessed by individuals who are thus freed from having to rely on the highly nuanced information generally supplied by both government and business. Scorecard can supply information on a localized basis as well as draft letters of complaint to be faxed directly to the polluter concerned and a copy e-mailed to the Environmental Protection Agency in Washington, DC. This kind of approach can produce puzzling and delicate situations for lobbyists who may find their favourite legislators bombarded with e-mail taking an entirely contradictory line to that proffered by their corporate clients.

So what are the political consequences of all this for states? The political loyalty of populations is generally given to individuals and institutions that are deemed to be effective agencies in controlling and moderating the effects of a basically hostile environment. This hostility might take the form of a natural disaster such as a major flood or an economic collapse, threatening prosperity and jobs; foreign affairs, in the form of invasion or attack; social or political dislocation and unrest, requiring immediate protective reactions. By the twentieth century all and more of these attributes were expected of a state and states, in various manifestations, were the object of most forms of loyalty and were generally able to deliver. The fate of the last Tsar of Imperial Russia or the demise of Reichskanzler Hitler indicated what might happen when they did not. These two particular events were made stark by the conditions of overwhelming conflict. What is happening now is the result of further evolution, rather than current conflict, though the technological advance which underlies it is the result of preparation for war, and the picture is perhaps fortunately less stark. The Tsar and, eventually, Adolf Hitler were replaced by new versions of what had failed and no one supposed it should be otherwise. But the replacement for the Tsar, the Soviet Union, has now itself collapsed, and the replacement for the Nazi regime in reunited Germany is in visible difficulties, as is the EU of which it is the principal member. What is going on?

Russia, the United States and the European Union

We can best get a picture by considering some examples: one comes from a state in continuing crisis: Russia. The initial collapse of the Soviet Union was itself instructive. The presence of political legitimacy in any state is and has always been the product of a domestic coalition of interests based on the belief that the abandonment of some particular desires, traditions and loyalties by each very local interest was worth it for the sake of the advantages conferred by belonging to the larger group. It was the collapse of this kind of coalition rather than the failure of Marxist ideology which ended the Soviet Union. Mikhail Gorbachev plainly recognized that the domestic system of the Soviet Union had ceased to deliver the social, economic and security benefits which justified its existence in the face of a multitude of particularisms – cultural, ethnic and religious – spilt all across the land from Eastern Europe to East Asia. He tried to reform it so as to deliver those benefits before their absence brought on disaster, but the system was too inflexible and too corrupt to reform fast enough and he failed. What followed has partly been the result of particular conditions and traditions within the Russian Federation, which in the face of faltering rule has had a historic tendency to go into a state of suspended political and administrative animation, until heaved out of it by some overwhelming event or ruler.

What is also interesting, however, is that it has seemed natural to an important group within Russia, and almost universally outside it, to replace the communist structure with economic and political versions of what had served the capitalist world well as a result of three centuries of development. It may be at least as significant in accounting for the fragility of democratic machinery in Russia and even more the utter collapse of any incipient free market economy – each made more or less conditions of outside assistance – that both notions arise from highly traditional ideas about what a state structure ought to be like. But if those notions are themselves now quite unreliable guides, they may be as outmoded as was communism. The combination of some unhelpful Russian traditions which, among other things, elevate the role of corruption and degrade the rule of law, with the effective imposition of structurally inappropriate mechanisms has had devastating effects on both Russians and their creditors alike. It is possible that Russia, more than any other state, may demonstrate with frightening clarity what is a general dilemma: how to adjust the institutions of the state so as to fit contemporary circumstances and swim successfully with the tide, when to do so could easily involve the effective dissolution of the national government as it exists and the evolution of an entirely new kind of entity; or whether to resist the tide thus courting public disorder and violent responses to it.

The United States, too, presents an interesting picture. Unlike the former Soviet Union, it is neither an existing nor the consequence of having been an empire in the past – that is to say, it is not an agglomeration of historically distinguishable ethnicities and societies, presided over or forcibly held together by a 'master race'. It has perfectly obvious social and ethnic divisions, but they were not created in the same way as those within the Russian Empire, and its profound geographical variations have not so far stimulated serious regional focuses of loyalty to match those of Europe or India. It is politically a genuine federation, already capable of devolution at any level required, determinable by constitutional practice. This last factor is already in use. Recent years have seen a reduction of federal power and a resumption of formerly yielded powers by individual state governments. The general notion of hostility to big government is easier to accommodate in the United States than almost anywhere else in the world. Nonetheless, the United States is not above the consequences of globalization. The position of the USA as the only remaining 'superpower' is complicated rather than triumphant and, even more significantly, is not the object of popular approval so much as popular puzzlement – a fact for which, during the 1990s the ruler of Iraq presumably felt grateful.

The constant pressure to be economically successful in the global environment is felt no less. In common with other societies, particularly the UK, there is anxiety about the quality of education because of an increasing sense of comparative failure in equipping students with the necessary intellectual tools of survival in the contemporary world. There is an almost morbid fascination with educational statistics expressed in terms of global comparisons. This is essentially because the degree of technological education present in a society has now become part of its ability to attract its share of the loose capital washing about the global markets. The result is a tension between the increasing poverty of governments whose tax base has been eroding and their certainty that more resources need to be put into education at every level. The responsibilities here have increased because of two major changes. The provision of education used to be based on the notion that there was a finite quantity required for individuals to function effectively in particular life roles. High school and college education, give or take some relatively small special skill – an extra language for example – would enable the newly minted adult to perform in almost any employment. Education was over and life began. No longer: this is impossible now in a world where the progress of knowledge is already rapid and getting faster. The rate of obsolescence in the high tech information industry – to name just the most obvious example – requires a continuous process of re-education. Meeting this need requires major revolutions in attitudes, to some degree already under way, and major expenditures.

What makes it a particularly difficult business arises from a second difference we should note. The educational systems of the developed world naturally reflect the practices and expectations of the past. In the past, education was seen to be part of a cultural training. It existed within a particular cultural tradition – French education was different from British, which was different from Russian and different again from American. The process acknowledged a local cultural past and contributed to a particular way of thinking about the present. Like states themselves, it was organized within and not above a society. To an important degree it taught you who you were in an individual cultural environment; as scientific education steadily increased in importance during the twentieth century, serious efforts were put into making sure that the scientists did not entirely miss out on this part of their education. Plainly, this aspect of education has to change. What the global economic system now requires is knowledge and expertise above and beyond the acquisition of intellectual skills and admission into the traditions and modes of thought of a single culture. Like communications, employment, banking and commerce, education has become de-territorialized. The special skills required to create the kind of global economic asset which it represents have no basis in any one traditional culture, and may be actually damaging to some of them, particularly in Asia. But no one who travels or has to deal with the rest of the world on a routine basis can escape understanding how far this development has already gone or that it will become ever more pervasive in the future.

Anxiety about employment has also been high and will resume when the present economic cycle moves on, and it springs from the loss of lower-paid jobs to the developing world and from a period of downsizing at corporate level, this last for reasons discussed in Chapter 2. The USA is certainly not immune from the deeply diffi- cult problems inherent in the falling price of labour worldwide, indeed, its internally high wage levels make it a potentially serious victim; nor would a protectionist tax and duty system do more than postpone the inevitable lowering of the USA average wage. The tra- ditionally autarkic structure of the USA economy has been super- seded by events and is beyond recovery; and its global trading imbalance makes it crucial that the USA remains an irresistible object of inward investment. These facts mean that the USA, like everyone else, has lost independent control of its economy. NAFTA, for example, is not a cause but a consequence of that change. Unlike everyone else, however, the USA has, because of its great size and traditional wealth, got much further to go in the essentially political task of creating public understanding and acceptance of what is happening and of the growing limitations on what the government, any government, can do. At the same time, the USA has acquired a crucial interest in the progress of the global economy generally. An Asian currency crisis, for example, and the consequential risk of an economic depression, is a USA crisis too, as was the Mexico crisis; and again in 1998, the potential for market meltdown implicit in the Brazilian financial debacle. Both supporting the global institu- tions involved and taking specific USA action have become crucially important political activities, perhaps more important in such cir- cumstances than any internal economic policy regulation could be – and matter as much to the prosperity of individual Americans.

The case of the EU is particularly interesting, because it, too, depends upon a functioning coalition of interests, but, like the USA, though in a different way, and unlike the Soviet Union, it delivers a great deal of what is required: but is it enough? Here is an area of high-level economic activity of great significance within the world's markets, the source of much technological invention, the origin of one of the most vigorous cultural systems the world has ever known and in general the provider of high living standards to its people. It has, with the exception of the UK, recently suffered from severe structural unemployment, endures almost unbearable pressure on the future of its social welfare systems from falling population figures and is making a pig's ear out of finding solutions to the political and security problems brought about by the collapse of the Soviet Union. It is also encountering a particularly difficult internal problem arising from a mismatch between the demands of the treaties which provide the basis for the further integration of the EU and the dwindling degree of popular support for them.

This aspect is of particular interest for this discussion. The provisions of the European Treaties from Rome (1957) to Maastricht (1992) and Amsterdam (1997) are based on a very important assumption, derived from the international circumstances of the first phase of the Cold War, namely that political and economic security were to be found, as they evidently had been for the past 75 years and actually were at the time, from creating a superlarge state. Europe was therefore gradually, or not so gradually, to become such an entity. Such a logic, particularly in good economic times, enjoyed popular support, and where it did not do so explicitly, perceived economic advantages provided alternative or start-up grounds for consent. The last expression of such an evolution is to be found in the Amsterdam treaty: here is the single currency, the Central Bank, the Defence Ministry in the form of the incorporation of the Western European Union, which would supply the common defence policy and the Foreign Ministry which would emerge from European Political Cooperation (EPC) to run the common foreign policy, both of which are required under the treaty.

These are the appurtenances of a sovereign, if federal, state and the effort to make them happen is visibly running into severe difficulties. The common currency is not inclusive, and, having proved initially weak, may eventually fail; the common foreign and security policy does not exist, and such success as EPC had enjoyed was dissipated in Bosnia and only recovered in part as a result of the war over Kosovo in 1999. All these things might be so because they are inherently difficult, and they are. But they are also in trouble because governments are encountering public objections, not just in Europeanly agnostic societies such as the UK and Denmark, but also in the former core states such as Germany and France, where a sense of loss of control coupled with persistently high unemployment rates has led to episodes of public disorder.

This development, coupled with the difficulties surrounding the process of enlarging the EU, which is also enjoined by treaty, might be interpreted as the result of the surviving strength of states and their persisting political legitimacy. A closer look does not suggest so. It is clear that publics do not see enough benefit emerging from sinking individual identities into a larger whole because larger entities are not doing well in the global environment. In this, their refusal to support the further integration of the EU mirrors the refusal of the old coalition of interests to support the continued existence of the former Soviet Union. It is also clear that within national states there is a growing suspicion that the erosion of sovereign economic management within states, which we discussed earlier, has made formerly highly significant areas of their activities increasingly irrelevant. The voting figures at elections steadily fall, complaints that the quality of both politicians and civil servants is in decline are sharper than they generally have been and there is a growing atmosphere of contempt for the institutions and sometimes formerly revered traditions of the state itself. This represents a decline in political legitimacy and it has been leading to an increasing provincialization. The focus of relevant activity, and sometimes a consequently revived focus of very old loyalties indeed, long submerged in the larger state for the sake of the advantages conferred by size, can often seem to lie in smaller units, substates, maybe, proposing significantly less sovereignty for themselves, but actually doing things that matter. This is not just a question of the revival of ancient loyalties – Scotland, Provence, Flanders, Catalonia, Bavaria would be cases of this – because in some cases functional regionalism has crossed boundaries hitherto divided by historical prejudice – at the head of the Adriatic and in the Tyrol, for example.

What looks to be required is something loose at the centre, having no pretensions to becoming a United States of Europe, which will draw up to itself just sufficient of the functions of the old state as will permit smaller entities to operate at the lower temperature that globalization has rendered appropriate. This would mean the end of the European state as it has been known for 300 years, and getting there involves reversing the vertical patterns of political legitimacy which evolved over that period and replacing them with broader bands of horizontal activities and supervising authorities. This cannot be done without creating or enduring a crisis of political legitimacy; nor can such a crisis be evaded by ignoring the tendency of public opinion and making a dash for full integration before it is too late.

It is particularly tough that this crisis is boiling up just at the moment when European governments – like all governments, but more obviously than some – have to find persuasive solutions to the more immediate problems provoked by globalization, most seriously those involved in the dismantling of the collectivist state in the face of the demands of the free market global economy, which will not invest where the conditions are too much restrained or made capricious by local state political decisions and policies. This means that the most unpopular and difficult choices have to be arrived at and implemented by governments who are already suffering the effects of creeping loss of legitimacy. Just at the moment that they need to be able to command the kind of loyalty that will absorb the shocks of highly damaging political decisions, generally only available in wartime conditions, they are losing authority. Here it makes little difference whether tough decisions are required to keep the traditional show on the road, as in France to enable the single currency to happen, or to respond to the globalized economy, as most obviously in Russia, Germany, India and China. These cases reveal clearly the gap that exists between what governments need to be able to do and what they now have the political legitimacy to bring about.

In using the example of the EU, we have something that is obviously very particular to Europe and it might be thought that the circumstances therefore offer no useful opportunity for generalizing. There are, however, enough signs of similar fissiparous tendencies elsewhere to give ground for believing that Europe is not in fact different but merely showing more advanced symptoms of the disease. The Russian Federation, India, Indonesia and China all present examples of the growing difficulties of managing large and to a greater or lesser degree ethnically complex agglomerations of territory, and any of them could have been used as evidence in this discussion.

The dangers in all this are patent: the breakdown of public order, examples already exist; the growth of extremist groups with a tendency to violent and terrorist activity, again examples already exist; the resort to aggressive nationalist rhetoric in foreign affairs or over questions of immigration and even the emergence of religious or quasi-religious sects, born of the abandonment of other kinds of hope and thus having a tendency to commit mass suicide. These are major and disturbing dislocations and they are evoking from politicians and other commentators exhortations to the resumption of former loyalties couched in the language of the past which sound ever more irrelevant. The biggest structural realignment of power in the world since the fall of Rome cannot be countered by supporting an increase of volunteerism in the USA or by exemplary shootings of regional tax collectors in China or by successfully – in the short term – striking to retire as a French truck driver at 55 on full pay. It is hard to tell governments that they must conduct research into the best methods of accomplishing their own retreat from the structures and attitudes of full sovereignty, but that is what needs to be done.

3
The Mechanisms of Global Relationships

3.1 Introduction

We have seen already the effects that globalization, particularly economic globalization, has had on the role and functioning of states. It has had no less an effect on the international system. This is chiefly because the international system with which we have been familiar for the last two and a half centuries has been a system of states – it evolved with them, served their purposes and developed principles, practices and organizations which reflected the structure and needs of its basic participants. With this understanding, we can trace the development of international and diplomatic law, the rules and practice of diplomacy, the making and breaking of treaties, the regulation of warfare, the emergence of international legislation on cross-border administrative issues and eventually the creation of the major international institutions of our own time. In general, the construction and functioning of this system have been one of the major human achievements in history, the equal, if not even the superior, of the invention of the state itself.

You have only to consider what is involved in making a significant international journey to see the point. When you enter an airport and even more when you enter a plane, you are protected by and subject to international safety regulations of enormous complexity. The qualifications for both air and ground staff who prepare and fly your plane are affected by international agreement. The rules about the use of passports and visas are also the consequence of international legislation. The arrangements for timetabling and

routing planes are made by an international organization set up
under treaty. The rights you have as a traveller and as an immigrant
or visitor are again internationally agreed, if not always observed.
The fact that English is worldwide the sole language of international
flight is the consequence of an international agreement, honoured
even at the height of the Cold War by all countries. Moreover,
we can add that similarly complex regulations exist to ensure the
smooth and effective exchange of goods carried by air, and that the
same thing applies to both people and goods when carried by rail or
road. In short, if it was not for a flood of legal and administrative
international regulation and cooperation, the routines of international travel and commercial traffic would simply not be possible.
This example can be paralleled in many other areas – controlling
disease is another good example – where it has been found convenient, and then customary, to have international legislation available to deal with the usual commerce between states.

These matters have been basically administrative and comparatively easy subjects for cooperation. When we turn our attention to
high politics and the systemic arrangements concerning the avoid-
ance and the conduct of war, as well as the making of peace, we find
that the texture is no less thick, but that the compliance level is
much lower. In these areas, states have wanted both to have rules
and to be able to break them when under extreme pressure – and
they have done so. Nonetheless, persistent efforts have been made
to organize international relations peacefully since the late seventeenth century, and since 1815 there has consistently been some
kind of formal or semi-formal organization whose task was to avoid
warfare and smooth the flow of international exchanges generally.
The European States System which, as the Concert of Europe, successfully managed affairs during the nineteenth century was succeeded after the failure of 1914 by the League of Nations, which
itself fell victim to the particularly hostile international circumstances of the 1930s. After the Second World War, the United
Nations succeeded it and continues to evolve. Each of these was an
attempt to learn from past failures and to meet the particular needs
of the moment and their individual characters reflect that combination. They will be discussed in greater detail in section 3.3.

In the twentieth century, these bodies have been joined by
the International Monetary Fund (IMF) and the World Bank. In

international trade, the General Agreement on Trade and Tariffs (GATT) has been recently succeeded by the World Trade Organization (the WTO) and regional economic organizations have multiplied, whether at low levels of operation such as the North American Free Trade Area (NAFTA) or the Association of South East Asian Nations (ASEAN) or at a much higher intensity, such as the European Union (EU). All these entities, whatever their purpose and constitutional character, are in one way or another associations of nation states and they exist to serve the reciprocal interests of national governments. It has become clear in the last ten years or so that, despite their complexity and prevalence, these organizations are mainly in decline. But, as we have seen earlier, there is as yet no effective way of speaking to let alone negotiating with representatives of the real sources of globally pervasive power: the information systems, global markets generally, private organizations and transnational companies. Unless and until centres of power such as these develop institutions and generate representatives, and organizations like the IMF agree to abandon their limitation to bilateral relationships, there will continue to be stresses and failures. It is obvious that the traditional international governmental organizations are suffering from weaknesses inherited from their progenitors. Associations of states do not supersede the state when it weakens, they share in the weakening process. The one possible exception to this – the EU – nonetheless shows some problems typical of the breed.

The evolution of complex organizations like these, particularly those that have been charged with maintaining peace, has been paralleled, sometimes induced, by changes in the patterns of warfare. Over the last four centuries, the conjunction of the emergence of more efficient and pervasive state governmental machines with a constantly improving technology of armaments turned making war into an ever more compelling exercise. What had once been the more or less casual conflict of the late fifteenth century became the 'total war' of the twentieth. With that a paradox developed: warfare became more and more terrible, but resort to war became less common, and episodes of war became shorter. The Revolutionary and Napoleonic Wars took over 20 years; the Second World War in its longest phase – 1937 to 1945 – lasted for eight. The control of war, however, demanded that its conduct remained firmly in the hands of all powerful governments. They might not be committed to peace for its own sake, but they were generally committed to acquiring and maintaining the approval of their citizenry, and the particularly catastrophic economic effects of modern warfare therefore represented a powerful restraining factor. What makes it important to discuss the changing patterns of warfare in more detail is that this restraint has become a declining factor in today's world, declining in a direct relationship to the relative decline of state governments. The result has been a sharp rise in the incidence of uncontrolled and often essentially civil conflict. This pattern of fighting has so far escaped any successful management either by governments or by their organizations, as the extreme difficulties encountered in dealing with the Kosovo crisis in 1998–99, among other episodes of the very late twentieth century, clearly demonstrated. It is a problem on the same scale as that arising from the emergence of centres of economic power which cannot yet be knitted into a global fabric of governance.

We will therefore look at the external consequences of globalization from four points of view: first, the changing role of states, secondly, the functions of organizations of states and private organizations, thirdly, the evolving patterns of war and fourthly the record of attempts to secure peace.

3.2   States

The machinery developed by states and their governments for handling external relations is inevitably being profoundly affected by the onset of globalization. Non-governmental organizations (NGOs) are equally profoundly affected and are discovering growing needs. In discussing the latter, we will use the term 'private organization' because the steadily increasing significance and range of what have been called NGOs make it perverse to describe them simply in terms of what they are not. These effects are further consequences of the emergence of areas of activity and power arranged horizontally across the globe which we have already identified. These either bypass or conflict with the vertically arranged structures familiar from the mid-seventeenth century onwards, but they do not supplant them, or have not done so yet, nor do governments and the creatures of governments show significant signs of actual demise, though in some cases they do show evidence of persistent and untreatable mange.

Put in the baldest way this means that the representative needs of governments have changed rather confusingly: they need less diplomacy of the traditional kind among themselves, but more of it, sometimes cooperatively set up, between themselves on the one hand and newer sources of power and influence on the other. To make the confusion worse, where the need is for more representation, it is not proving to be adequate to try to redirect the existing system, the structure itself is having to be modified. For the new areas of activity and power, the need is at least as difficult to meet. There is little or no tradition of representation and in many cases no structure which could evince it. A process of evolution is thus beginning, reminiscent of that which flowed from the evolution of the sovereign state in seventeenth-century Europe and eventually developed all the subtleties of the traditional inter-state diplomatic system. While new mechanisms are forming, a crisis is occurring which arises out of the vacuum caused by the natural inability of even reformed representation of the old style to engage with new methods of representation that are simply not yet there. We can divide these effects into those bearing on states, where important changes are occurring in what is regarded as 'foreign' policy and in the machinery for constructing and deploying it. Secondly, there are the effects on existing inter-state and private organizations, where the effective withdrawal of governments from some areas of international activity has imposed the need to create new representative functions. There is also the converse effect on new areas of activity which exude power and influence, but so far have yet to go any significant distance along the road to self-representation.

To begin with states: the consequences for governments are far-reaching. They range from the great question surrounding the outcome of the squeeze on governments coming from both above, from regional trading groups for example, and, in Europe, from the expansion of EU powers and from below, from provincialization and regionalism, where thoroughly local loyalties seem more useful than giving allegiance to any larger unit. This is the question mark that hangs over the locus of political legitimacy at least in economically developed states. The process is much less advanced elsewhere, a fact which has stretched quite sharply the differences between types of states and creates further uncertainties. In time, the levelling effect of the global availability of information and services may work to the advantage of currently less advanced states and in some Asian examples is already doing so: but for the present the wide variations remain a difficulty and, in any case, it is not clear that the ability of less developed societies to leapfrog some technological hurdles will result in any permanent levelling of the playing field. The administrative duties of governments have also come into question. Familiar patterns of admired and powerful bureaucracies, difficult to enter, well paid and secure, carrying out public administration with lesser or greater degrees of political management are being dismantled. The general demise of the collectivist state is one reason for this, but the increasing inability of governments to impose a high tax regime and remain in power is another. To apply deregulation and competition to the administrative organs of the state has seemed an obvious path to take both on principle and to save money.

Of all areas of government activity, the most susceptible to this kind of argument have been the foreign and diplomatic services. It is perhaps instructive that these were and have traditionally been felt to be the senior and central activities of the fully sovereign state; it is they who have been the first and primary casualties of contemporary developments. Diplomacy had become the sole preserve of foreign ministries and foreign services by the early eighteenth century, with the exception of China, which resisted the notion for a further century. Events in the international system and the behaviour of governments confirmed that concentration until the First World War. After the war, the cumulative effects of expansion of government roles and activities, which had begun before the war but were very greatly emphasized during its course, began to break down the monopoly of foreign ministry control. The profound significance of economic policy for governments, and its use, in the form of economic sanctions, as a weapon intended to achieve international coercion, gave to financial and economic departments of governments a newly independent role in managing international negotiations and transactions, particularly in the field of tariffs, reparations payments and loan repayments. The same tendency could be seen with respect to disarmament negotiations which were required by the 1919 Settlement, but ultimately failed. The first obvious sign of the change came with the exclusion of foreign ministries from the negotiations between European powers, but most specifically Britain, and the United States concerning the status and repayment schedules of the war loans.

This tendency continued without any great acceleration until the 1960s when two factors began to produce rapid and dramatic change. The first of these occurred in Europe where the progressive establishment of the institutions and functioning of the EEC/EC/EU began to establish new patterns of inter-state activity among the members. This activity was derived from a relationship that was still international but also incipiently federal, and the latter element created a need to have direct relations between individual departments of state, defined not by nationality but by topic. Strengthening the process, the same effect was simultaneously required in the relationship between individual governments and the central administration at Brussels. While the most striking evidence of the trend was to be found in Europe, other pressures appeared more widely. The operation of the IMF, the World Bank and GATT – eventually the WTO – as well as other economic and development matters, sometimes handled through the UN system, provoked similar changes across many countries, as did the highly complex negotiations, requiring a very particular kind of expertise, which were necessarily involved in attempts to control the nuclear arms race.

The foreign services of states were not only the victims of structural changes, they had also been the victims of a precipitous decline in reputation after the First World War, when people suffering from the catastrophic effects of the war felt that they had been betrayed by diplomacy's failure to prevent it. There was some recovery during the Cold War, but their perceived role declined again thereafter, at least in the field of 'high politics'. An atmosphere of exclusivity, of foppish luxury and increasing irrelevance clung to them, however unjustified. The reasons are not hard to find. In a world where the imperatives of global politics seemed to be almost entirely economic and commercial, what part could a cultured generalist play? In a world where nuclear catastrophe might be prevented by arms control agreements, it seemed that only expert negotiators could possibly make them. But most damaging of all, in a world where the acquisition of information and the exchanging of messages had become both easy and generalized, the traditional duty of foreign services to put their government's view in the most effective way and to send back up-to-date information from their mission seemed to have been scooped by the new communications system. In a deeper sense, the duty to guard the basic security of their country as a sovereign entity was eroded as the world situation was itself transformed by globalization, transforming at the same time the meaning of the concept of national security. All these factors reduced public and political willingness to continue to support the traditional diplomatic services.

Moreover, as the number of issues on which governments and non-governments needed to speak to each other both expanded hugely and became more technical, the range of administrative services across which they were spread also vastly increased. There is a similarity between the way in which governments have found the need to talk to each other at levels other than just the top and not confined to the use of a single point of entry and exit – the foreign ministry – and the way in which government departments within a country have also found that the issues they have to process demand cross-ministry treatment at almost any and every level. It is a lesser example of the same horizontalizing tendency so obvious in the world at large. Within the EU, of course, the tendency is compounded by the necessity for each ministry to deal directly with Brussels, thus subtracting a major part of the political role of embassies of member states within member states, never mind their respective foreign ministries. Consistent attempts to prune and reduce expenditure on what was increasingly regarded as a perhaps unnecessary and certainly unnecessarily luxurious foreign service have scarcely been surprising.

In common to some degree with the defence services – and to be seen, too, perhaps in doubts about the future role of NATO – the response has been a remarkable effort to escape from the atmosphere of luxurious secrecy and exclusivity and to find a new role for foreign ministries and diplomatic services, sufficient to give them relevance in the context of globalization and the effects of the communications revolution. The first gives rise to great efforts to broaden the basis of recruitment, to embrace fully all the technologically advanced systems available for both communicating and publicizing the work of the service and to insist that all officers, however senior, must acquire such skills. There is also a tendency to reduce staff wherever possible, to abandon, where it existed, the idea that representation should be almost universal and that where it does occur it should not be too comfortable either in terms of accommodation or allowances. Economizing in this respect would be imposed by the general reduction in public finances and major efforts to achieve savings by better use of technologically advanced equipment and making imaginative arrangements for the leasing of embassy buildings and the sharing of compounds can be found in many foreign services. So, too can multi-accreditations. Embassies are affected in other ways as well. They, too, are no longer hierarchically arranged extrusions of the foreign ministry. They have become a house of 'many mansions' in which widely varying national operations, groups, organizations can find an office from which to conduct business. The huge increase in travel and migration in recent years has been important in this because of the way distressed nationals have extended some aspects of the remaining welfare state on to the diplomatic and consular fields. The ambassador becomes a kind of chairman of a multiply sectored company, or as has been suggested, a version of the senior partner in a law firm. Such reforms are useful as well for image-altering purposes. In fact, the latter purpose has been, perhaps unexpectedly, helped by the all too real dangers and privations caused by highly unstable conditions in many parts of the world. Respect for diplomatic immunity and the ancient taboo on harming accredited diplomatic messengers do not survive where most sending governments no longer have or would wish to use the long arm of forcible retribution, and where the perpetrators of atrocities need have little fear of the doctrine of reciprocity.

A second part of reversing past negative images involves becoming much more open about the formulation and management of policy with legislatures and the media, both of whom have often felt excluded, as well as with the public at large and more precisely with groups interested in external affairs either for historical, economic or intellectual reasons. These groups can be offered an entry into the process through advisory committees and academics are being much more extensively consulted in their areas of expertise. In addition, there is a growing tendency to introduce 'revolving door' schemes whereby secondments can be arranged from and to private civil organizations, chiefly in the fields of the environment, human rights and humanitarian aid. Thus a general sense is spread that external policy is at least to some degree a cooperative enterprise, based on inclusivity and accessibility. The process goes further than trying to erase the negative perceptions of the past. Finding positive roles to play is even more important. Strict attention to what a country's interests and needs actually are and focusing on them to the exclusion of any more general ambitions has been a feature of the process. The result is usually that overseas services are to be concentrated on areas of actual or potential economic interest, the neighbours, the major global institutions and wherever there might be a national diaspora. In these areas, diplomatic activity though accomplished with highly advanced communication techniques, is of a recognizably traditional kind, basically bilateral except where institutions are concerned. In addition to this trimmed role, there is the newer importance attached to public diplomacy. Public diplomacy, particularly in its cultural form has long been seen as an adjunct to the diplomatic exercise, but generally inferior in significance to the high dramas of inter-state political rivalries, and its practitioners regarded as less than 'real' diplomats. This is changing in contemporary conditions and particularly in the light of the all-pervasive influence of the media, including discussion on the Internet. Sometimes it can feel as though there are two quite separate worlds involved – the real one and a contrived virtual version created for the media by the actors involved. Skill in achieving this has added a new whiff to the very old odour of mendacity which has always hung about what the representatives of governments may say.

Public diplomacy means paying close attention to creating and maintaining good opinions held about one's country by the public of another. The hope is that the government of that country will be responsive to the fact that its public generally supports the aims and general stances of the government diffusing such public diplomacy so that in a crisis or a prolonged negotiation friendly attitudes will prevail. Thus all kinds of contact, ranging from sporting fixtures through cultural tours to newspaper articles or radio and TV coverage, are of potential significant promotional value. A broadly favourable view of a country – for example that it is honest, efficient, compassionate – may also affect the likelihood of global business locating itself in one country rather than another. Depending on the degree of development of a country, public diplomacy may also involve forms of aid – direct or indirect, for example, medical or educational respectively. Humanitarian disasters of one kind or another also provide opportunities for public diplomacy at many levels and sometimes, occasionally, a form of public diplomacy in itself, by cooperating, amidst fanfares, with a humanitarian civil organization. Public diplomacy is open to the charge that it is propaganda by another name; but it is not propaganda put about in the interests of control and it very definitely does not have the field to itself. If it was not basically correct, the global information system would provide a quick means of being found out and discredited; and in any case it has to compete with the pervasive orchestra of attention-seeking noise to be found on the Internet which again puts a premium on being both accurate and useful.

The development of public diplomacy also emphasizes another feature of the contemporary foreign service. As in so many areas of activity both government and non-government, the pyramid of authority is being flattened by the nature of the work to be done. To achieve good negotiating positions on particular issues, to relate successfully to issue-based global organizations and meetings as well as to formulate successful public diplomacy, there has to be a wide range of connectivity: within the service – across departments in the ministry and between embassies and the ministries, and very possibly other ministries. Outside the service there have to be connections with politicians and interested groups, often national and global civil organizations, other friendly governments and, crucially, business and finance. Plainly priorities of this kind have implications for initial training and subsequent staff development.

It remains for discussion to what extent this development responds to a real need and is effective in doing so and to what extent it is a self-preserving invention. For some countries who carry a heavy load of historically important remembered activity, but who have been just as affected by the erosion of state roles and the global diffusion of power as everybody else, the construction of public diplomacy is both an attempt at shedding the load and a device for tracking the extent to which it is reducing. Forming policy for public diplomatic purposes in the inclusive way generally suggested and increasingly implemented can also be seen as in itself a way of recreating a national identity in a new image for domestic purposes as much as foreign. It is almost as if the role of a state has shrunk so much domestically that it is to be defined by the external perception it induces, and that the very activity may be crucial to its survival. As to the effectiveness of public diplomacy in creating a global basis of support for the general mores and specific points of view of a country, the jury will be out until time has provided more experience.

One reason why this is so is that in the rush of information and communications overload and in coping with the unstable nature and movement of power across the globe and, not least, the sheer pace of technological and political change, logical thinking about what foreign, global or external policy is actually for is hard to do. States originally had foreign policy in order to counter threats before they led to invasion or some other war and to find and maintain alliances both for that purpose and to support the waging of war if that proved necessary. They came to limit their relationships to the outside world to those conducted officially through the one point of entry or exit, the foreign ministry, or through commerce. They did so in a conscious effort to identify and defend themselves against credible threats occurring in a society of states arranged in a vertical relationship to each other, just as they maintained internal administrative machines arranged similarly. In a period of transition such as is occurring now, elements of that situation survive, chiefly among less developed states and societies, but also in certain parts of the world – North East Asia for example, and the Middle East, including the Gulf. But these are not typical. What constitutes a threat has to be completely differently considered in the context of horizontalized activities. In one sense these activities are themselves extremely serious in their damaging effects on the structure and role of states; however, this is not seen as a threat, except in some economic and financial matters, because the effects of globalization have on the whole been beneficial to individuals in economic terms and particularly to individuals in terms of personal empowerment. The individual as beneficiary of the information revolution is not inclined to want to defend a homeland against it, until isolationary protectionism seems a plausible defence against uncomfortable economic restructuring, at which point the disadvantages of doing so may seem as clear as or clearer than the advantages.

The real threats are not those traditionally seen as arising from abroad and aimed at the security of states as such, but to personal security. They arise from horizontal areas of power often thus far at least uncontrolled or restrained by a human agency. Job security, security from electronic or other transnational crime, cultural security, security from terrorism, security from environmental degradation and, in some areas, security from complete administrative and political breakdown and the consequent humanitarian crisis: these are the real threats. Here the mongrel nature of contemporary foreign policy becomes obvious. Few if any of these categories are specifically foreign, each is in fact a mixture of domestic and foreign, involving some aspects that are globally common to all states and domestically cross the traditional frontiers of administrative responsibility. One consequence of this is the appearance of the argument that the main function of a foreign ministry is to act as the coordinating element in the generation of national policy responses to regional or global activities. Such coordination will go beyond government and include other national groups or interests and may even also involve coordination with outside bodies. Thus far, though certainly some signs of this appear, coordination seems to be moving towards presidential and prime ministerial offices, as the complications involved require such political authority for their resolution that only the most senior political centre can provide it. The end result of this process may be the concentration of the remaining high politics function of foreign relations at the apex of the system, while leaving large quantity, lower level coordination to foreign ministries who may come to suffer from indigestion as a consequence.

All of these considerations suggest that, in developed states at least, any doubts that may be felt about how to answer the question 'what is foreign policy for?' and 'for what should foreign service officials and diplomats be trained and retrained?' are not signs of intellectual or political weakness, but accurately reflect the acute difficulties of operating in a transitional situation. The key to understanding the problem lies not so much in a process of constant reduction, reform and 'rebranding', which cannot be ends in themselves, but in watching for the moment when the new global centres of power either acknowledge and improve their representative systems or, if they lack them, generate them. When that happens dialogue between the possessors of power will again be possible and become the most immediately practical way to deal with potential and actual threats to citizens. State governments may be downsized, but they will not go away; they may find themselves in a far larger company of entities than they ever supposed possible, but they will still be there. And they, like their new interlocutors, need to talk and they will need structures and staff – diplomats – to do it for them. Their already expanding willingness to face global problems with an interdisciplinary range of skills and people is a necessary start. More tangible results will await the arrival of other parties with whom to engage, but it is for that they must prepare.

3.3   Inter-state and private organizations

However much the diplomacy of governments tries to adjust to new conditions, the effort is limited by the effective absence of 'the other side'. The conduct of relations between states may well be transformed, but it is only part of a picture. In more recent times, further factors of great force have emerged. The need to face and try to resolve the great questions surrounding the fate of the global environment has created mixtures of the highly political with the professionally scientific which require profoundly different authors of international exchanges from those of the past. If previous pressure had served to blur the familiar lines of responsibility for international negotiation between and within states, these new areas of activity look set to erase them altogether. More than that, they involve establishing new relationships between state governments and the private entities which have created highly significant roles for themselves on environmental issues, seeking and obtaining political support for their activities transnationally. Little about these developments is entirely clear and there could be no successful attempt yet to describe them definitively; nor are these episodes of diplomacy involving both states and non-state entities completely effective. It is an inevitably muddled, if fascinating, area. The relationship, however, between the UN and UN agencies and private actors in the humanitarian field generally has quite clearly changed. The effect of the series of world conferences on economic and social issues which occurred during the 1990s made insiders of private actors who used to think of themselves as outsiders. Both in planning agendas and in forming delegations, private actors came to take leading roles, and the UN found ways of bypassing bureaucratic restrictions on the process. In effect, flowing from the accreditation of 1400 private organizations for the Rio Conference on Environment and Development, a new layer of recognized participants in the global political order has been created. A new world of diplomatic activity has thus been created for both old and new actors.

In order to try and get a closer look at what is actually happening on the ground, we need to identify particular occurrences which are reasonably frequent and develop characteristic patterns of behaviour. Since the end of the bipolar system after 1989, such an exemplar has emerged in the form of humanitarian intervention. The immediate reasons for this are twofold and can be more simply stated than can their fundamental causes: the bipolar system rested on a creative tension which pushed the leaders of both poles into action of some kind or another if the domestic affairs of a country or a region began to run out of control. What they did was not always either desirable or effective, but there was no doubt about their willingness to react. Since the end of the bipolar system, that willingness has largely evaporated. Without the needle of international tension, societies – and therefore, their rulers – have been unwilling to make sacrifices of money, resources or men and women, in order to maintain domestic or regional order elsewhere in the world. The potentially serious regional destabilization caused by the Kosovo crisis in 1999 eventually led to a military response by NATO, though not from the UN. That military response, however, involved no direct casualties on the part of the NATO allies and this fact was frequently alluded to in satisfied terms. Secondly, this evolution has come side by side with a marked increase in the number of crises caused by the collapse or near collapse of nation states. All states have suffered a diminution of both internal and external authority in the face of the pressures of the global communications revolution, brought about by the magic combination of telephones, orbiting satellites and computers. The overlapping webs of human activities which have resulted have served to erode the spiritual and practical bases upon which the nation state was predicated. At the upper end of the scale, the result is nervous discomfort and uncertainty, at the lower end, it is disaster and collapse. The mixture which seems to assure global security at the level of inter-state relations but leaves it desperately threatened within many societies and polities, has left major potholes and broken bridges in the highways of global relationships.

The major questions that arise are these: where the internal administration of a state to all intents and purposes disappears, who will provide it, either while reconstruction proceeds, or while something completely different evolves? When the consequences of collapse produce tribal, gang or economic warfare and/or brigandage, who will stop it? When these events produce utter disasters for human beings – no food, no water, no housing, the break-up of families in refugee camps, the spread of disease, episodes of murder and rapine – who will relieve the suffering? In what order should help, if it is available at all, be provided? Whose duty is it to set priorities?

Plainly one often supplied answer to these questions is the United Nations system. It has, however, become perfectly evident that the UN system is not capable of dealing with these problems. The reasons are not entirely straightforward; emotional rhetoric sometimes serves to conceal natural limitations on what can be done by referring only to the need for rooting out corruption and adopting administrative reforms. Achieving either of these will not change the fact that the UN is an association of states and, as such, shares in the disadvantages that the contemporary world has dealt out to its members. This makes many expectations of what could be achieved wildly over-optimistic, and returns us to the questions asked above.

The answer, as events have unfolded, has been that the only practical source of help – however woefully inadequate the circumstances often make it – has come from private organizations, most often from the great charities, such as Oxfam and Médecins sans Frontières (MSF), both of whom have graduated from local to global status, and also to a wide variety of other private actors, specific in origin by country and by activity, and large in numbers. The reasons go beyond the nature of the problems on the ground. State collapse renders the traditional way in which other states have responded irrelevant: a bilateral approach and the consequent use of bilateral diplomatic and other machinery become useless. The same, even more awkwardly, applies to the UN. Dealing with the government of a state is the only proper manner for the UN to operate, and if there is no government in effective existence the mechanisms of the UN run into formal difficulties. The most likely solution can be to put the UN into a coordinating role, with all the weaknesses that implies, so that it can arrange to operate through deliberately established or pre-existing local and international private actors. For governments, there is another motive over and beyond evading the problems caused by the failure of bilateral relationships. In a post-collectivist atmosphere, the direct use of tax revenue to relieve external humanitarian disasters can be politically infeasible: the 'privatization' of humanitarian efforts relieves this problem. The free market in humanitarian feeling – and the contributions which flow from it – allow private charitable actors to multiply. They then become available to governments as the recipients of funds delivered in a competitive environment, and influencing their activities permits the pursuit of policies which might not – probably would not – have been tolerated by an even partly effective domestic government. For both intervening governments and the UN, this is particularly true of human rights issues, but is not confined to them.

The result has been an impressive shift in the route by which resources reach crisis areas, as private actors have increased their share of the financial action. In 1970, 1.5 per cent of the income of private actors was derived from public grants; in 1996, it was probably over 40 per cent. In 1992, some 13 per cent of overseas development assistance from the industrialized world was being channelled through private actors and the amount has risen since. Such flows have inevitably caused a change in expectations as to how much private actors must contribute from their own resources before being entitled to matching funds. In some cases, deliberately created organizations are being 100 per cent funded from public sources. Such inflows give influence to the donors and particularly where the intention is to find substitutes for direct intervention, the donors expect performance and behaviour consistent with developed models. This contributes to the tendency of private organizations not only to supply the administrative functions of dead states, but to conform their own organizational structures to the patterns of 'Western' state institutions.

At a basic level, organizations founded and funded on the basis of a transcendent, sometimes essentially religious, desire to give aid and comfort to individual human beings in distress find themselves involved in something almost infinitely more complicated. The simple river of both intention and intended actions runs out into a complex delta of slow-moving muddy channels, difficult both to map and to navigate. The principal problem is deciding how to apply the practical help to individual sufferers when no infrastructure – even a primitive infrastructure – any longer exists. Thus it has to be decided to what extent it is the proper function of private actors to provide the prior conditions in which help can be effectively given. There is always then a further problem in a seemingly never-ending chain of difficulties: providing anything other than direct assistance to individuals carries a political message of some kind or another to one group – usually armed – or another, and therefore creates the risk that the best of intentions may be being used for less good purposes either accidentally or deliberately. And this complication may go further than the local political and administrative morass. It may involve the wishes and policies of state governments, most likely neighbours, but also possibly others hoping to have influence from further afield. In such circumstances, the private actors concerned may find themselves divorced from the kind of neutral status maintained by the Red Cross, whether justly or not, and thus put themselves and their staff at risk of attack and assassination. People who have volunteered to serve in such circumstances have always accepted a degree of risk, but becoming potential participants in warfare has not generally been seen as that kind of risk.

The point about raising these issues – and the list could be very much longer – is to show that, to the quite remarkable degree that private actors have taken on new roles in current humanitarian crises, they have acquired a different relationship both to the crises themselves and to all the other parties also involved. These are generally four: the remaining sources of authority in the state concerned, other states, public and other private organizations. States have no problem being represented at the scene, and public organizations, particularly agencies of the UN, also have little problem with representing themselves. For private actors, however, there is a problem. Little in their traditional activities has prepared them for the need to represent themselves or to become involved in coordinative negotiations, but both are having to be done on a daily basis. MSF field directors and coordinators, for example, can find themselves functioning both medically and politically – particularly in respect of relations with the media. So crucial can this aspect become that staff can be seconded to almost purely political activities, as has happened in respect of the MSF Nairobi Coordinator since 1992, with responsibilities for relationships with local actors both in the Horn of Africa and in Rwanda and Burundi. When the going gets really rough, as with the abduction of MSF staff in Chechnya, a small group of four people was drafted from line management positions and acted for four months as a negotiating agency with local power brokers in order to secure their release. Similarly in Georgia, where civil conflict has become endemic, the Red Cross has intervened in the educational system by providing instructions in the laws and conventions of war in the hope of providing a more secure background against which humanitarian work can be carried out. It is a very striking testimony to the current problems of some states that a private organization should adopt the schools not to inculcate the idea that killing is wrong, but that it should be made more acceptable in its form and be confined to the local population.

These changes have been both dramatic and painful for many. At one level, with which we are not so concerned here, they have produced internal crises of principle, particularly about the degree to which private entities should participate in raw politics. On the ground this may mean coming to terms with the fact that helping one party in a domestic breakdown may enable it to further its own ends in a situation where those ends may involve both violence and corruption. This is an inevitable consequence of humanitarian crises arising out of state collapses rather than natural disasters of one kind or another, and it greatly complicates the act of doing good. In some cases, it can lead to a private actor withdrawing from a position where it either knows or fears that it is being used by particular players in the game for their own political advantage. On the broader field of global politics and responses, the character of the events that follow a state collapse usually, probably always, involves serious violations of human rights. How far humanitarian private actors ought to become active in the publicizing of such violations as part of their contribution has been and will remain a subject of major controversy. When these controversies are resolved in ways that extend the role of private actors, they naturally affect their activities. The combination of attempting to avoid serious misuses of their assistance by benefiting parties and the frequent need to provide administrative and infrastructural services as the major part of humanitarian assistance results in the need for complicated

diplomacy in a very obvious way. Warring groups must be negotiated with, both as to their own behaviour and their willingness to
tolerate the presence of the private actor and, equally important, as
to their relationship with other groups and other sources of authority – the remains of a state, for example. In order to make administrative and infrastructural assistance effective, decisions have to be
agreed with at least five – it can be more – potential other participants: the existing structure, to the degree that it remains, warring
factions seeking power at the centre, or secession from it, other private organizations, often many in number, several neighbouring
states and multiple organs of the UN system. And the need for negotiation is further complicated by the rising number of participants.

The levels of activity also represent a thickening weave. The level
might be medical – both staff and supplies, food provision, environmental – essential services, such as water supply, military (which
brings with it the whole issue of achieving and maintaining a minimum degree of security), or the need for urgent administrative
action, with all the attendant questions of relevant political authority. All these characteristics are producing changed requirements
for the officers of the private actors involved. A new emphasis on
obtaining staff with professional and political skills is emerging, coupled with the provision of training. Comprehensibly, the familiar
short-term use of essentially amateur officers is giving way to longer-
term contracts for professionally qualified personnel. Through the
mists of these changes, accelerating as they have over the last five
years, can be seen the emergence of staff members who, having
joined a private humanitarian organization on the basis of enthusi-
asm and the possession of one basic skill – in a branch of medicine,
for example – find themselves turned by experience, and sometimes
by actual formal training, into perhaps unwilling but nonetheless de
facto diplomats and administrators.

There is also an interesting paradox, another among the many
that globalization brings, in that much of the work that private
organizations and branches of the UN system do in collapsed states
is designed in the first place to cope with the consequences of collapse and fill some of administrative holes so that immediate assistance can have some effect. In the longer term, however, it is
intended to bring about a restoration of the ability of that state to
resume governing itself. At a certain level, the UN, in particular, is

still investing in the idea of the national state, regarding its problems as a blip on the graph and capable of resolution. To the extent that an ongoing role for the state is certainly present in the contemporary global economic environment such an attempt is justified. To the extent that such an ongoing role is much reduced from what it once was and that fact represents one of the causes of collapse, the attempt to restore a state's function may simply fail over time, or look like a building permanently encased in scaffolding. Bosnia-Hercegovina, and probably Kosovo in the future, are cases in point.

The increasing involvement of private actors in human rights – over and beyond those whose business they are – is creating the need to generate another kind of diplomacy: creating public pressure on governments and sometimes companies. To bring effective pressure to bear involves not only local action but, just as significantly, attempting to move major governments into action both separately and through the UN system. This may need to be done quietly, or noisily, in direct contact with legislative committees and foreign ministries, or it may be done by attempting to influence public opinion on a national and transnational basis. On a general basis, ICVA (International Committee of Voluntary Associations) does this in Europe and on behalf of Third World private actors and InterAction operates similarly in Washington. In addition, private actors usually in coalitions have moved into the lobbying business. Sometimes this is done, particularly by smaller and perhaps 'one issue' actors by ensuring that events involving them on the ground are substantially reported by the media. Larger and more permanent actors have concluded semi-federal agreements, whereby they retain independence of action but cooperate for the purpose of winning power and influence, with consequential allocations of resources. This is particularly significant in respect of UN and EU funding and the division of labour involved smooths the process of negotiation. The existence of a part-time MSF Liaison Officer to the UN since 1983 is a case in point. MSF has also felt the need to have an office in Paris whose task is to supply a steady flow of reliable political and contextual information about areas where the organization is involved, or might become so, based on research involving economic and regional expertise. In these cases, activities, and staff to run them, are required which are far removed from the original purposes of many private actors whose stock-in-trade was the provision of emergency aid to individual human beings caught in a disaster.

The thickening texture of communication between private actors and the pre-existing machinery of the international system is a mark of the breaking down of the hierarchy of international significance. The role of private actors is more nearly equal with that of states and institutional groupings of states, like the UN. The role of their staff has followed suit. The importance of the private organizations' perspective in political forums has been demonstrated by its increasing relevance in official delegations or in humanitarian cells in capitals. A former senior manager of MSF heads the 'humanitarian crisis reflection cell' of the French Ministry of Defence, a former Oxfam executive is the key official dealing with humanitarian issues in the UK's permanent mission to the UN, to which may be added the September 1997 appointment of Julia Taft, then President of InterAction to be US Assistant Secretary of State for the Bureau of Population, Refugees and Migration. Moreover, in November 1997, Roy Williams, Vice-President, Overseas Policy and Planning of the International Rescue Committee, was appointed to be Director of the US Federal Government's Office of Foreign Disaster Assistance. The representatives of private organizations are routinely included in official delegations to General Assembly sessions and special conferences. Revolving-door assignments also are widespread between private sector and UN positions, particularly in operational programmes such as those of the United Nations High Commissioner for Refugees (UNHCR), United Nations Children's Fund (UNICEF) and the World Food Programme (WFP), where there is a tradition of picking talent from private organizations. In many ways these links between non-governmental and governmental spheres of activity are a novel feature of the UN scene, impossible to imagine a decade ago.

There can be no doubt that we are witnessing the development of a new layer in the global diplomatic system, evolving from major changes in the machinery of global politics. It is more than a quantitative change. However easy it may be to point to the presence of private actors with influence on international politics in the past, both the level and the manner of its contemporary application have altered in a qualitative way. The balance of power among the entities involved has shifted – away from state governments and associations of states and towards private actors. To set against this, it is to be remembered that some of this change has occurred because the new entrants are acting as surrogates for governments. They do so in circumstances where traditional bilateral relationships cannot survive a state collapse or the objections of domestic public opinion to interventionist policies. Nonetheless, to be used as an agent requires both being present and being able to deploy particular advantages; and for both purposes self-representation is essential. The historically familiar problems arise about whether, however morally right it might seem, it is effective to rely only on expressing the opinions and requirements of an organization. Taking the time to discover all that can be found out about another party's own situation and thus knowing what the political practicalities are, takes the representative activity rather further, but can be extremely valuable. Should 'liaison' officers be two-way channels of information using it with some discretion, or are they messengers only? In many ways, the internal organizational travails, the messy external associations and the multiplicity of very different and differentially powerful entities in the system, with concomitant confusion about status and role, are extraordinarily reminiscent of the early phases of the states system. The Pope and the Holy Roman Emperor would have sympathized with the plight of the Secretary-General of the United Nations, the King of Spain with the President of the United States and Cardinal Richelieu with the chairman of MSF International, as would so many harassed toilers in the field of humanitarian intervention with the dangers and indignities of representing anything or anybody during the worst of the Thirty Years War in early seventeenth-century Europe.

3.4 New areas of activity without organizations

The globalization of manufacture, of commerce, of finance and of information is open to widely varied interpretations of its significance, just as is the exact degree to which governments are losing out to global forces they cannot control. Put at its minimum, however, what has occurred is highly significant, significant enough to have engaged both public anxiety and supplied individual opportunities. It suggests at least two paradoxes: the possibility of narrowing the economic gap between developed and less developed societies

yet the plain risk that it may in fact be widened; that changes in
public policy have been induced yet the effect of those changes is
severely limited. These paradoxes arise out of the parallel existence
of older sources of authority and areas of economic and financial
activity which are not new in themselves, but which are newly
arranged across the globe in layers. The result has been that familiar –
yet always difficult – methods of making the ebbs and flows of such
economic activity as controlled as possible have become not just difficult but ineffective. The annual global Davos economic summit
discussions both in their very existence and in what topics they
review are further evidence of the need for new developments, but
do not add up to any viable systemic response. The need for some
moderating mechanisms has become more and more obvious,
particularly where the uncontrolled movements of the unsleeping
global stock and currency markets and the global banking system
have brought instability to regimes and ruin to individuals. Similarly, there is increasing pressure for putting some limits on what
dangerous or perverted information can be purveyed via the Internet. This last is separate from the desire of some governments to
control the Internet for reasons of domestic security or to protect an
ideology.

In general, where governments have attempted to assert control,
they do not succeed very well. Carrying out occasional cooperative
sorties against currency speculators can have temporarily satisfying
effects, but mainly even when governments cooperate, there is
somewhere else in cyberspace for their chosen victims to go and the
game carries on. Most widely accepted regulatory regimes in any
field have occurred, and then been tolerated because they meet a
need and what was convenient became customary. Higher motives
have generally been offered after the fact. In present circumstances,
it might be expected that initial chaos and the wringing of governmental hands would give way to some signs that the new areas
of economic and financial power conceived and born out of the
physical and temporal freedom of activity conferred by instant
global connectivity, would discover the need for self-generated and
self-policed limitations. For that, cooperative structures would be
required and thereafter – and only thereafter – the possibility of self-
representation would arise. As yet, global issues discussed by the representatives of global authorities have visibly begun to develop in

the areas already discussed. Representation has not yet emerged elsewhere. This is why the remarkable efforts to reinvent diplomacy which states are making has not so far evoked an effective response. One set of cogs is ready to engage, but some of their doppelgänger are not yet there and it is not yet possible to slide into a new gear: hence the sense of irrelevance or flailing about which can emanate from the machinery of global political exchange. The effect is familiar to historians of diplomacy: this what it felt like to be the Pope trying to deal with a Protestant government and perhaps even more sharply with a Catholic one strongly jealous of its sovereignty or, later on, the Emperor of China attempting to explain their proper role to European states. If representation is not yet possible, if, for example, the IMF cannot speak to the representatives of currency speculators – Mr Soros unfortunately being unable to acquire accreditation – are there at least signs of some internally generated structures arising?

The Internet provides some useful examples and well illustrates one of the most difficult problems involved. The need to administer the Web has led to what has been termed the Web's unelected government: the World Wide Web Consortium (W3C). It has attracted the complaint that it is too secretive for a group that effectively sets social policy in cyberspace. The consortium, which is based at MIT, is an international collective of 275 companies, non-profit organizations, industry groups and government agencies that was created to set technical standards for the Web. For a group of such significance W3C is not well known. Its critics argue that the consortium, whose meetings are private, should open itself to broader, more democratic participation. Although the consortium's first decisions involved nothing more controversial than which codes should be used to create web pages, it has quietly strayed into areas of social policy. The two most striking examples of such activities are PICS, a series of codes designed to help parents screen out objectionable material while their children surf the Net, and P3P, a system designed to protect privacy on line. The constraints of more open participation would be antithetical to W3C's charter as an industry body, responsible first to the needs of its funding members.

Further evidence emerged in January 1999 when the first meeting of the Global Business Dialogue took place in New York. Its basic message was clear: the rules of electronic commerce were not to be made by governments alone. Convening on the 44th floor of the Bertelsmann Music Group building in Times Square – far from Washington or any national capital – the assembled captains of the media and technology industries agreed to prevent conflicting governmental regulations from obstructing business in cyberspace. Instead they planned to devise their own united policies on such issues as on-line privacy and taxation under the umbrella of the new organization. Those attending included Bertelsmann AG, Time Warner, America Online, IBM, Netscape, France Telecom, Fujitsu and Toshiba. Recently, therefore, it has become possible to give some affirmative answers: the stock markets, the global banking system and the Internet itself all show signs of generating self-supervisory mechanisms, operating horizontally. Naturally there is a long way to go before they send forth ambassadors, virtual or otherwise, not least because some kind of accommodation across vertical and horizontal lines will have to be made with governments, and that process could yet be a battle royal. But perhaps for the first time, there is actually a route map for the future. The whole mechanism of global exchange and negotiation is following the movement of power and gradually falling from the vertical to the horizontal. States have responded first, as has been seen, and existing globally operating institutions are also doing so, in varying ways and responding to differing stimuli. Both of these groups had and have reformable structures. The most direct beneficiaries of globalization have profited initially from having no structures; but the process has now gone far enough to be able to discern the emergence of new constructions arising out of new concentrations of power and influence. When they begin to talk to each other and to want to join in the game with the other players already waiting on the field, a new global system will be in place, accurately related to the centres of actual power. They will generate representatives of some kind and for those whose bent and intentions give them both the wish and the qualifications to be diplomats, the world will quite literally be their oyster.

3.5   Evolving patterns of war

However the new institutions for managing the economic and political affairs of the world develop, they will be powerfully affected along the way by the changing patterns of warfare. These patterns have, unsurprisingly, been formed in a close relationship with the shifting structure and role of the national state. It is unsurprising because during that period the principal agents of warfare in recent centuries have been rulers and governments, and what affected them also affected their willingness and relative ability to wage war. What globalization has been doing to states is reflected in what is happening to both the incidence and the conduct of war. That warfare is undergoing particularly important changes in today's world becomes very clear when they are set against the historical record. What follows gives such an account. The first major change of the twentieth century came with the First World War of 1914–18 and one at least of the major actors involved – the British Foreign Secretary, Edward Grey – was aware of its significance:

> We are going to suffer, I am afraid, terribly in this war whether we are in it or whether we stand aside. ... I do not believe, for a moment, that at the end of this war, even we stood aside ... we should be in a position to undo what had happened in the course of the war ... and I am quite sure that our moral position would be such as to have lost us all respect.

So said Sir Edward Grey to the British House of Commons on the fateful afternoon of 3 August 1914. It was not quite the argument for joining the conflict that the French Ambassador at London – Paul Cambon – might have hoped for. Earlier in the day he had been discovered in the Secretary of State's anteroom by the Head of the Foreign Office – Sir Arthur Nicolson, Harold Nicolson's father – who politely enquired why he was there. 'I have come', he blisteringly replied, 'to know whether honour is still a word in the English Dictionary.' The difference between the two points of view is deeply instructive. The Ambassador, who was a good and intelligent man, believed that wars occurred because treaty obligations had been broken and a formal *casus belli* had thus arrived. The consequential war would rapidly and antiseptically right the wrong that had been done – specifically in this case the invasion by Germany of Belgium, a neutral state. He further believed that not only was Great Britain in duty bound to defend Belgium, but also to come to the aid of France, with whom military planning for just such an eventuality had been taking place since 1906. Edward Grey, on the other hand, who was also a good and thoughtful man in the fullest sense, but not of a quick intelligence, had nonetheless grasped a fundamental change both in the nature of international politics and in the likely course of a war. When he returned from the House of Commons to the Secretary of State's office overlooking St James's Park, he collapsed against the mantelpiece groaning to Arthur Nicolson: 'I hate war, I hate war.' The following morning, still at the Foreign Office, he saw the lamplighter pass along the Horse Guards dowsing the street lights, and made his most famous observation: 'The lights are going out all over Europe; they will not be lit again in our time.'

He was of course abundantly right. He had been British Foreign Secretary since December 1905, and he had come to understand that there had been a sea change in the scale and objectives of international policies. He had to ask himself often what the intentions of the German Empire were, what the emerging economic power of the Russian Empire meant and whether the vigorous hatching out of US power was in danger of creating an undefeatable enemy for the British. He was the first Foreign Secretary to have to live with the fact that after the Anglo-Japanese Alliance of 1902 and the defeat of Russia by Japan in 1905, there was an ineluctable global international system, in which nothing could happen anywhere that did not affect everyone everywhere: Britain had enjoyed many private hiding places, now there were none. In a global international system, power had to be conceived globally, and that fact sharply reduced the number of serious players who were automatically qualified to play in the game and induced corresponding insecurities and ambitions in those who had to win in qualifying rounds. The first group consisted of Russia, the USA and the British Empire – the last only temporarily – and the second consisted of Germany and Japan in terms of ambition, and France in terms of insecurity. At some point the qualifying rounds would begin and, when they did so, huge areas of territory would be involved and the massive armaments which, responding to the lethal combination of deep insecurity and major technological advances, had been steadily building up since the turn of the century would create warfare both more destructive and on a larger scale than anything hitherto seen.

For some commentators, the economic disaster that would follow was so obvious that they drew the conclusion that no government would any longer be able to go to war. For the reason that Grey had given to Parliament, all would be destroyed – guilty, innocent, participant and neutral. At a turning point like this, however, many more simply thought about war by reference to the last one involving major powers that was commonly remembered; and that was the Franco-Prussian War of 1870. It had been brief, decisive and although followed by the Commune in Paris, it had not seriously involved society as a whole. Previous nineteenth-century wars had been even less immediate in their effects on ordinary people. So despite the unnoticed indications which did emerge from the Balkan Wars of 1912–13 and the Russo-Japanese War of 1903–05 of what contemporary war on a large scale might be like, all governments in 1914 found themselves dealing with popular emotions which owed little or nothing to rational expectations and a very great deal to the new and rabid popular press. For them, circulation figures could be easily boosted by running nationalistic and bombastic headlines for weeks at a time.

Pre-Napoleon

It was to take the course of the First World War itself to reacquaint emotion about warfare with its reality; and in a while we will use contemporary poetry to help us to understand what happened. First, however, we should take some notice how warfare had unfolded in earlier periods. Generally speaking, warfare was sharply constricted and localized; it used weapons, which though they slowly advanced in sophistication, remained remarkably primitive. It was focused on precise ambitions or the defence of quite limited possessions or influence. Wars were also limited by campaigning seasons and the demands of agricultural production. They formed the stuff of heroic literature and legend, and were accepted as unpleasant, but nonetheless potentially romantic. Compared with the period since the Renaissance, centres of political authority might be impressive, particularly culturally, but they were seldom able to administer internally or act externally efficiently or consistently. Some, particularly phases of the Chinese Empire, did demonstrate those characteristics and succeeded in raising and using large-scale forces. But the activity of warfare remained remote from most citizens, and the Chinese notably retreated from the chance of establishing a general military superiority when they inexplicably abandoned both gunpowder, which they invented, and large naval vessels, in which they once reached East Africa, in favour of rigid isolation.

The emergence of better organized state governments during the sixteenth and early seventeenth centuries also led to more destructive warfare, particularly in the use of cannon to destroy fortifications hitherto correctly deemed impregnable. Such a weapon in the hands of centralizing rulers was an important asset. The weakening of local lords was also a factor leading to a decline in virtually constant local conflict and a narrower concentration on major civil wars, wars between rulers, both of which, during the Reformation period, were aided and abetted by ideological division. The effect of the joint arrival of personal firearms in addition to cannon and profound religious conflict led to the most damaging war of early modern history. It was the Thirty Years War and it was fought over a wide area largely in Germany and Central Europe with significant repercussions elsewhere; 1998 marked the 350th anniversary of its end. Some of its episodes of savagery introduced a new standard and gave it a general reputation: its atmosphere is wonderfully caught in Bertold Brecht's play *Mother Courage*.

The consequences of the gradual emergence of the sovereign state which we noted earlier, included the opening of the period of state domination of international politics after 1648. The effect was to complete the restriction of warfare to that waged by states. Partly as a result of the new kind of entity that states were becoming, the objectives of warfare also changed. The role of a military conclusion in the determination of ownership of territory became more important than ideological victories or the acknowledgement of a particular place in the pecking order of monarchy. The growing significance and thus cost of administration played a significant part here: to establish title to a piece of territory carried with it both opportunities for taxation and the obligation to bring advantages to the ruled. For both ruler and ruled, clarity over where borders ran was a matter of great importance, and there was a noticeable trend for the treaties of the late seventeenth century – and ever thereafter – to include clear maps delineating ownership. These were acknowledged by the appearance of frontiers physically marked out on the ground.

By the end of the eighteenth century, the distinction between being at war and not being at war, which had always been ceremonially marked but was in practice usually not at all clear, became much more precise, partly because states were finding that the expense of raising and supplying large armies and navies, which was now very plainly their direct responsibility – there were no more shadowy hirings of Sir Francis Drake by Queen Elizabeth I of England – was not much to their taste. Wars became a last resort, embarked upon after diplomacy and threats had been exhausted. Our knowledge of their causes, their dates, the treaties marking their ends and the conditions imposed or achieved is very complete and used to be learnt by heart on pain of dire physical punishment for failure. The Duke of Marlborough, King Louis XIV, General Wolfe and General Washington, and many others became almost personal acquaintances.

Napoleon

The tendency of rulers to avoid war because of its disruptive effects domestically and its expense did not survive the French Revolution. From 1792 until 1815 war was waged almost continuously some-where in the world. It was not the first war to have a non-European dimension, but it was the first to integrate the two almost com-pletely. It is quite possible to argue that during the Seven Years War (1756–63), the non-European elements – chiefly in India and Canada – were regarded by the participants as a separate enterprise and that the eighteenth century in general was prepared to have conflict overseas without thinking that necessarily meant that the parties must also fight in Europe. Nonetheless, the French Revolu-tionary Wars were genuinely centred in Europe and on a scale never before seen. The fighting at various points raged from Ireland deep into Russia and from Portugal to Denmark. As we noted in the con-text of political legitimacy, it marked the return of ideology as a sig-nificant fuelling element in two ways: it made ethnicity a serious part of the justification for the existence of a state and thus sancti-fied nationalism as a creed and it promoted the idea of the liberty of man, though not, of course, either the idea of equity in the condi-tion of men or the principle of representative democracy. The result was a unique struggle between the Revolution, initially adopting Napoleon as its agent, and all the force the power of its ideas could engender both within and outside metropolitan France and, on the other side, the concerted opposition of the other major rulers. The conflict seemed endless: coalitions rose and fell, but never accepted the apparent result of military defeat by Napoleon. Napoleon planned a great European imperium in the tradition of Rome and Charlemagne, even adopting their clothing styles in grand theatrical gestures, a habit wonderfully caught in the great portrait of him by Ingres, but he could never build reliably on the apparent security given by military victory. He was an instructive example of Lewis Carroll's idea of the need to keep running in order to stay in the same place.

This instability reflected a fundamental mismatch in the foundations of power on the two sides. In terms of the realities of power, France was no more powerful throughout the war than any of the other major participants. This was not a rerun of the Louis XIV period nor a precursor of Germany 1897–1945. France was the beneficiary of the international force of the ideas unleashed by the Revolution, particularly in the negative effects that they had on the security of regimes that rejected them. Napoleon, until he became Emperor, was able to profit from and build on this fact. Equally, his opponents were able to sense that the domination of Napoleon could be rationally challenged in terms of military power and would not give up. He was thus able to divide them, defeat them temporarily but unable to get a lasting settlement. Once the Empire began, both the title and the measures that Napoleon increasingly took to defend it, caused him to lose credibility as the standard bearer of the Revolution and forced him back on the intrinsic resources of France. Opposition to the domineering Emperor of the French grew, encouraged by the war of attrition being waged by the British aiding Iberian nationalists in Spain, and in response to the Continental System.

This last was an extremely interesting development and represented Napoleon's definitive weapon against the British. Like many things about the period, it was both extremely old fashioned, yet familiarly modern. Napoleon came to recognize after 1801 that Britain could not be negotiated with, invaded or defeated at sea. The source of her resilience and the funding for successive coalitions against him, was her growing economic primacy based on the flowering of the Industrial Revolution. Napoleon believed in the eighteenth century doctrine of physiocracy – that all economic power was rooted in the land and its products. In this prescription, economic power located in commerce and banking was essentially ephemeral and thus vulnerable to attack. The chosen method of attack was a kind of reverse economic sanctions: Napoleon ordered the whole European market to be closed to British goods and services, and his military machine set about enforcing the ban. The results were predictable: British economic dominance was rapidly transferred to the rest of the world, where it became total and Europe fell into a desperate economic depression, while of necessity importing otherwise unobtainable goods from Britain, secretly, against Napoleon's proscription. The Dutch began to complain that Napoleon's regime made grass grow in their market places, and the Tsar of Russia refused to enforce the rule. In 1812, Napoleon responded to that obduracy by invading Russia and thus embarking on the downward path that ended in abdication in Paris two years later. It was the moment of truth: the exercise of military might based on an insufficiency of purely French power was not adequate to hold and defend the Empire against the objections of its non-French population and the economic primacy of the British. The naval war was lost first in 1805, the economic war gradually after 1809 and the European war between 1812 and 1814.

Many features of the Revolutionary Wars were familiar: the constant attempt by Britain to prevent the construction of a single great empire in Europe was both well established and to be continued – perhaps it still is; Napoleon's attempts to recreate an old notion of the essential unity of Europe largely by using the pre-existing ideas of the Enlightenment and the overwhelming significance of sea-power are also unsurprising. The scale of the war, however, was impressive and was widely regarded by contemporaries as calamitous. Nonetheless, it is worth remembering that there were many parts of Europe where the war rumbled only distantly or not at all. In England, the novelist Jane Austen wrote all her major work during the war, and not once does it appear as any part of the context of her novels. It may also be worth remembering that when the war was over, Napoleon thought that he would be allowed to become a country gentleman in England and live some 20 leagues from London. When it was decided to exile him, if only as far as the island of Elba just off the western Italian coast, the reason for doing so was partly that he had behaved in a barbarian manner during the war. There had been a brief moment of armistice following the Peace of Amiens of 1801. The English gentry immediately resumed their habit of continental travel, particularly the Grand Tour to Italy, and were thus caught abroad when the war also resumed almost immediately. Napoleon interned them all instead of following the usual practice of letting them return home because they were civilians and thus not directly involved: this was held to be an unforgivable barbarity. Where we see more significant change, however, concerned the nature of Napoleon's power. After him, no state could again be ruled solely on the basis of a legal right conveyed by inheritance: popular consent and obedience to the idea of the nation had entered the equation and the nineteenth-century state was to develop such cohesive power that it eventually, in conjunction with other technological factors, changed the nature of war.

1914 to 1945

The point at which this became clear was 1916. The nineteenth century was quite remarkably a period of orderly international relations, effectively managed by a committee system of the great powers, usually mediated through conferences. There were occasional interruptions, generally caused by nationalist ambitions, and the system did not function outside Europe though, after 1856, the Ottoman Empire in Europe was included, and after 1884 Africa as well; but, nonetheless, it was a remarkable achievement. The principal war of the period was without question the American Civil War and its lessons, both strategic and political, might have been better learnt had it been less far away and internalized. The most obvious lesson would have concerned the effect of industrialized technology on weaponry, and in the sense that all governments began to be concerned about keeping up with a technological race in armaments, it was learnt. In the sense that there were consequences for the conduct of war on the participants which might make warfare less palatable to those citizens required to fight, it was not. Nor, as was observed earlier, did any general sense diffuse that in a rapidly growing phase of interdependent economic activity, large-scale warfare would inevitably induce massive economic disruption.

The fatal combination of factors which dictated the structure of the First World War has already entered our discussion under earlier headings: the nineteenth century saw an unprecedented upward shift in the efficiency and ingenuity of industrial technology. This impacted on state governments in advanced societies in the form of popular expectations that what improvements now lay within the power of governments should indeed be achieved. To do so required a large increase in the scope, size and expense of governance, which in turn led to increased taxation and recruitment of government personnel. This made the politics of governing much more immediate than before, since doing so involved a far greater use – and possible abuse – of power. This factor was much advanced by the coincident emergence of the tabloid press, able to speak to a public newly literate as a result of educational improvements and compelled to do so by reason of competition in the most lurid and simplistic fashion. The power inherent in political office went sharply up just as, simultaneously, the security of incumbent governments declined in the face of the fact that both achieving power by winning elections and then staying in power were more difficult than they had ever been. The combination produced government by propaganda – though in differing degrees – in all advanced societies, whether fully democratic or less so. And nationalist propaganda was often a successful distraction from domestic criticism, which might not matter too much if the external world was stable, but became highly dangerous and risky if it was not.

By the 1890s the international system of the previous century had effectively broken down. Technological improvements had created a new and global basis for assessing and using power and changed both the field of activity and the names of some of the players of the game, which was uncomfortable enough, as we saw at the outset. It had also had a predictably improving effect on the destructiveness of weapons. The machine gun – the Maxim gun, particularly – had produced a category improvement during the second part of the century. Improvements in the technique of rifling were by 1900 producing cannon capable of delivering destruction over many miles. The German Big Bertha was the apotheosis of all such guns: it was possible for the Germans to bombard Dover docks in England from bases in northern France during the First World War. Nor was transporting weapons of this kind difficult in principle. Big Bertha was arranged on a special train and could be sent anywhere a train could go. Therein, however, lay a highly significant restriction. All militarily sensitive areas in Europe were served by strategic railways; indeed, one of the bases of the Franco-Russian alliance of 1894 was that French capital would build strategic railways in western Russia to help defend the Tsar's Empire against any German threat. Those lines

were mainly built in what is now Poland and later came to be a welcome resource of the Soviet Union, whose attitude to France was
rather different. The restriction was, of course, that no amount of
military planning, however obessively engaged in as it was, could
ensure that a war would actually take place where the railways were.
And that meant that at least for the time being, armour, though it
had to be the best available, was still no substitute for infantry.

The reverse occurred at sea. Fitting a steam engine into a ship
increased rather than decreased its range and manoeuvrability. By
placing the most advanced guns on ships powered by the most
advanced engines, an almost perfect weapon was produced. As insecurity developed and the arms race hotted up in the early twentieth
century, naval competition ceased to be measured in terms of numbers of ships, but more in terms of technological advance and future
capacity. Planning and procurement based on assessments of the
building capacity of potential enemies were a new development,
which had devastating consequences for arms expenditure and
could seriously skew, as it did in Imperial Germany, the formulation
and management of economic policy. It also made general staffs
extremely reluctant to risk their high-tech babies in actual battle.
The First World War was almost devoid of naval engagements, and
the one serious battle – Jutland – was inconclusive in its result. The
uncertainties inherent in the naval situation greatly embittered
Anglo-German relations, led to the Anglo-French naval sharing
agreement of 1912, which meant that Britain could no longer be
neutral in a European war, whatever weasel words might be used to
cover up the fact, and generally contributed to public anxiety. Few
matters were so much the object of inter-state press abuse during the
period 1901–14.

On land the effect of the technological situation was to be disas-
trous. The railways could not provide the manoeuvrability for the
most advanced armour that ships could, and there would remain a
tactical gap until the invention of the petrol engine made enough
progress to be applied to the transport of big guns. There was thus a
pause until in 1917 the first tanks came on to the field – to remain
there until our own day. To those who have driven a great tank in or
out of action, or watched them streaming across whole countries in
what seems like an unstoppable lava flow, the sense of awe will
never quite go away and leads to reluctance in accepting that guided

weapons systems have sharply reduced the need for human guides encased in impregnable armour-plate.

What was significant about 1914, however, was their absence, not their presence, because it was their absence which immobilized the war tactically and killed millions and millions of combatants in the trenches. In the face of a tactical stalemate, the only recourse was to outperform the enemy in size and numbers. To win required more men, more weapons, more ammunition, more barbed wire, maybe more allies, than the enemy. To win also required more economic organization, more domestic planning and most important of all, more political stability than the enemy and more than anyone had ever had before. The tactical and strategic failure and the consequent losses were staggering. Harold Macmillan, Prime Minister of Britain from 1957 to 1963, a decorated officer who survived the First World War, once broke down and wept during a TV interview while trying to explain that only the terrible slaughter of cleverer and better men than he had allowed him to become Prime Minister. The scale of the conflict was different from all predecessors and it produced the justification for Marx's observation that wars do not change things, they merely make things happen faster. State machines that had already expanded hugely during the second half of the nineteenth century had to become almost totally invasive in order to conduct the war. Economic organization, the rationing of food supplies, the management of transport systems, almost total control of labour were all required. Although serious bombing of civilian populations was to be more of a feature of the next war, there was no branch of civilian life into which the effects of the First World War did not penetrate. Of them all, the most serious was the necessity of persuading and then compelling the able-bodied male population to go to the trenches to be killed. This task required not only organization, threats and penalties, it required a justifying motive. The propaganda machines went into action on a scale never before seen and never forgotten since. It was urged that the cause was just, the country and or the Empire must be defended, the enemy was wicked as demonstrated by atrocities committed. But these did not work in the face of continuously worsening slaughter. Few people in Western Europe or the USA are left who experienced it. For others, the experience of subsequent wars, though unpleasant enough, simply cannot equal the enormities of what happened in France in 1916 and 1917.

To make the point in a different way, here are two different poems to compare: both justifiably famous. The first is by Alfred Lord Tennyson and it describes the Charge of the Light Brigade during the Crimean War (1854–56). The charge itself was a pointless error committed by an incompetent general. The second poem is by Wilfred Owen and apart from the vivid description of being gassed, it is his utter rejection of the idea that it is meet and proper to die for one's country – which is the meaning of the Latin phrase at the end of the poem – which was so important and so dangerous for governments. First, the *Charge of the Light Brigade*:

Half a league, half a league
Half a league onward,
All in the valley of Death
Rode the six hundred
'Forward the Light Brigade!
Charge for the guns!' he said:
Into the valley of Death
Rode the six hundred.

'Forward the Light Brigade!'
Was there a man dismay'd?
Not tho' the soldier knew
Someone had blunder'd;
Their's not to make reply,
Their's not to reason why,
Their's but to do and die:
Into the valley of Death
Rode the six hundred.
Cannon to the right of them
Cannon to the left of them
Cannon in front of them
Volley'd and thunder'd;
Storm'd at with shot and shell,
Boldly they rode and well,
Into the jaws of Death
Into the mouth of Hell
Rode the six hundred.

Flash'd all their sabres bare,
Flashed as they turn'd in air
Sabr'ing the gunners there,
Charging an army, while
All the world wonder'd:
Plunged in the battery-smoke
Right through the line they broke;
Cossack and Russian
Reeled from the sabre-stroke
Shatter'd and sunder'd.
Then they rode back, but not,
Not the six hundred.

Cannon to right of them,
Cannon to left of them,
Cannon behind them
Volley'd and thunder'd;
Stormed at with shot and shell,
While horse and hero fell,
They that had fought so well
Came through the jaws of Death,
Back from the mouth of Hell,
All that was left of them,
Left of six hundred.

When can their glory fade?
O the wild charge they made!
All the world wonder'd.
Honour the charge they made!
Honour the Light Brigade,
Noble six hundred!

And now the Owen:

Bent double, like old beggars under sacks,
Knock-kneed, coughing like hags, we cursed through sludge,
Till on the flares we turned our backs
And towards our distant rest began to trudge.
Men marched asleep. Many had lost their boots

But limped on, blood-shod. All went lame; all blind;
Drunk with fatigue; deaf even to the hoots
Of tired, outstripped Five-Nines that dropped behind.

Gas! Gas! Quick, boys! An ecstasy of fumbling,
Fitting the clumsy helmets just in time;
But someone still was yelling out and stumbling
And floundr'ing like a man in fire or lime...
Dim, through the misty panes and thick green light,
As under a green sea, I saw him drowning.

In all my dreams before my helpless sight,
He plunges at me, guttering choking, drowning.

If in some smothering dreams you too could pace
Behind the wagon that we flung him in
And watch the white eyes writhing in his face,
His hanging face, like a devil's sick of sin;
If you could hear, at every jolt, the blood
Come gargling from the froth-corrupted lungs
Obscene as cancer, bitter as the cud
Of vile, incurable sores on ancient tongues,
My friend, you would not tell with such high zest
To children ardent for some desperate glory,
The old lie: Dulce et decorum est
Pro patria mori.

By late 1916, none of the traditional justifications for the privations and casualties of war would any longer suffice. The only
mantra which still had some force was the idea that this war had to
be won in order to end all wars and, less directly described, that
those who had been involved were entitled to and would obtain a
new social and economic order at its end.

There was no doubt that there were two contradictory effects arising from the experience of the First World War. The first was that
the traditional liberal state had been nearly bankrupted both literally and figuratively by the experience. In Russia, it was supplanted
by another way of attempting to manage an industrial, or in this
case, industrializing, society which overtly and deliberately accepted
the absolute superiority of the state machine and relied upon the

Communist Party to make it work equitably. A little later, fascist movements developed, first in Italy – perhaps significantly in the hands of a former Marxist – which also accepted and glorified the machinery of the state and relied upon a mixture of corporatism, patriotism and economic success to make it work to the advantage of a particular society. Both found to a greater or lesser degree that maintaining full control of the machinery of state was essential, but tricky, and required the use of major propaganda weapons and ultimately terror. In the United States, Great Britain and France, but not in Japan, the liberal state survived, but in the case of the European states, only just, and in all cases by increasing the role of government to almost wartime proportions. The second effect was that war as an instrument of policy either as threat or fact became, understandably, totally unacceptable to public opinion in all major countries and much reliance was initially placed on the League of Nations to make the maintenance of peace a reality. This meant that when the first effect of the war produced fascist regimes which began to lose their reluctance to go to war in a miasma of national propaganda derived from stereotyped memories of ancient Rome or the glories of Valhalla, there was no stomach to resist, no willingness to rearm, little attempt to plan for the unthinkable.

Moreover, the unthinkable had now become, if possible, worse. The First World War had produced the first serious use of air power in war, but it had not really included bombers or bombing. The British then advanced the technique rapidly by using bombing with outstanding success against rebel Kurds in what was then the mandate of Mesopotamia, now Iraq. Military planning could no longer ignore the significance of air power. Ironically, it was a clever young French staff officer called Charles de Gaulle who in the 1920s produced the first description of what, taken over by the Germans, was to become known as blitzkrieg: that is to say the combination of rapid movement of light armour on the ground accompanied by punishing and coordinated raids from the sky. The vivid film footage of the Japanese attacks in China, the German invasion of Poland on 1 September 1939 and the attack across northern Europe in 1940 all attest to the force of the technique. That side of air power reinforced the fact that, unlike the previous conflict, the Second World War was to be mobile as far as the battlefield was concerned.

The other side of air power, however, which had made the unthinkable, if possible, worse, concerned the civilian population, and they could not be mobile. The civilian population had suffered both by privation and the death of family members and had certainly been profoundly affected by the First World War; it had not, except rarely, been directly attacked. That immunity was shattered in the summer of 1940, when the Germans opened an undeclared war against neutral Holland by utterly destroying the city of Rotterdam in a sequence of bombing raids. It was not, however, unexpected. From the early 1930s onward a catch phrase developed in defence circles which read 'the bomber will always get through' – meaning that however many fighters were sent up to intercept fleets of bombers enough would survive to flatten the major cities. This belief, which was only wrong in that it overestimated the scale of destruction, at least until the bombing of Dresden in 1945, helps to explain both the reluctance to abandon any chance of negotiated settlements that seemed to be on offer and the policy of arranging for the instant evacuation of children from major cities into the countryside on the outbreak of war. The fear of total bombardment also included the idea that civilian morale would not survive it, again an overestimation. In neither the British nor the German case did that prove to be true. Indeed, it tended to have a reverse effect, which was later to be seen also in Vietnam. The deliberate attempt to break the nerve of an enemy population, rather than just defeat its military forces or undermine its economy, was the hallmark of the Second World War, and it ushered in the period of 'total war'. The phrase predates the invention of nuclear weapons – though of course they made it even more true – and it completed the process begun between 1914 and 1918 whereby the combination of state power and advanced weapons technology created wars which had to be fought on every front – military, civilian, economic, social, ideological and technological. Nothing that mankind could invent or process was not grist to the mills of war.

The Cold War and after

The Cold War offered a curious juxtaposition. The threat of war had become nuclear and therefore total in the completest possible sense, but barring accidents or insanity it also rendered great power war less likely to occur. And, more than that, it made small conflicts less likely to escalate, though it increased the fear that they might. Even after the production of so-called tactical nuclear weapons, the threat of war did not increase, as it became clear that the weapons concerned were regarded as more nuclear than tactical. It is possible to argue that nuclear weapons in fact made little difference to the fundamental distribution of power in the world, since their emergence coincided with the final conclusion of the great struggle for global power and influence on the part of the truly global powers. Once they had reached a de facto accommodation, which they did at the Geneva Conference of 1955, the armaments situation, though dizzyingly dangerous in itself, was a confirmatory factor rather than a fundamental one. A subtle change in the function of the intelligence industry reflects this. From the early twentieth century onwards, intelligence was used to try to discover war plans and technological improvements in weaponry: to steal a march, if possible, and to prevent one being stolen. With the onset of the bipolar era, it became crucial that each side should know as precisely as possible what were the forces and equipment available facing it and a pretty clear idea of the use to which they would be put in the event of war. Intelligence was there to defend developments in train, but allow them to be known about as soon as they were ready for use. If the stand-off did anything directly, it served to make it less likely that the two great powers would intervene very much outside their groupings to initiate or profit from events affecting smaller states. This became particularly obvious both in successive phases of the Arab–Israeli conflicts, particularly 1956 and 1973, Indo-Pakistani and Sino-Indian wars and after decolonization produced other broad areas of instability, for example, the Congo in the mid-1960s. Minimum intervention was applied in order to maintain the status quo as far as possible, and to that extent the existence of organized blocs of allied powers had a generally restraining effect on the conduct of international politics.

It now begins to look, however, as if the chief effect of the period of bipolarity was to restrain the outbreak of domestic disorder within states. Neither during the period nor since 1989 has there been any great tendency for inter-state or inter-alliance warfare to develop, or for the extraordinarily high-tech weapons systems that have been generated to become actors in themselves, in a 'man as a prisoner of the machine' syndrome. But there has been an almost catastrophic decline in the domestic security of many states, and some have disappeared into maelstroms of civil war. Nobody knows what to do about this and as it is at least likely that the late twentieth-century economic collapse in Asia may underscore this effect, as the late twentieth-century crisis over Kosovo in Yugoslavia has also done, the point is a significant one. The effect of this factor on the conduct and incidence of war is clear. The incidence of war is greater now than it has been since the seventeenth century, but the level at which it is being conducted is lower than anything seen so far in the twentieth century. We now observe the extraordinary paradox that the world possesses at least the remains of the most sophisticated means of fighting a war, both in weaponry and communications that has ever been known, yet the purpose for which it was all so expensively put together has disappeared, leaving the weapons stocks, the control systems and the alliances strategically and emotionally directionless. The objectives of those who wish to fight or support fighting have become localized and low-tech weapons generally more than suffice. Disorganized groups, more perhaps like brigands than armies, roam medievally throughout the forests and mountains of parts of Central Europe and the Caucasus, glad to acquire a rifle, willing to launch grenades from hilltops into market places below. Still more familiar from early modern Europe is the rapidly mounting list of accompanying atrocities and there is plenty of evidence that it is getting ever more difficult to shock ordinary people with accounts of recently perpetrated violence. Burning at the stake was once, too, considered perfectly normal.

The extraordinary crisis which came to a head in the Kosovo province of Yugoslavia in 1998–99 exemplified these factors. The crisis was essentially caused by a state collapse, that of former Yugoslavia after the death of Tito and the demise of the Soviet Union. The creation of newly independent states out of its ruins also created new minorities and non-negotiable disputes which unleashed appalling atrocities, first in Croatia, then in Bosnia-Hercegovina and finally in Kosovo. In Kosovo the basic cause of the descent into civil war was the fear of the Serbs that the province of Kosovo would seek and obtain independence, since its population was in large majority Albanian. The Serb government first revoked the autonomy of Kosovo in 1988, and then ten years later, having been defeated in the long crises over Croatia and Bosnia, sought to

avoid a third humiliation by violently enforcing Serb control over
the Albanian population, who had by now acquired their own resistance movement in the form of the Kosovo Liberation Army (KLA).
The civil conflict got steadily worse and both parties committed
atrocities, but because the Albanians were the majority ethnic group
with 90 per cent of the total and had enjoyed autonomy in the past,
the brutal nature of the Serb attempt to defeat the KLA and restore
order and its effective sovereignty in the province, apparently by
forcing the Albanian population to flee, strikingly offended external
opinion. Great efforts were made to negotiate a cease fire and an
acceptable return of autonomous status for the province, and in
early 1999 it seemed that the Rambouillet Conference, held near
Paris, had achieved that aim. At the last moment the Serb government rejected the draft agreement, and the NATO alliance began to
use massive air bombardment on non-civilian targets in Serbia in
order to force Serbian compliance with at least a version of the
Rambouillet agreement. After a much longer period of bombing
than had initially been anticipated and, significantly, only after serious preparations for a ground war were put in hand, the Serbs gave
way. But even in apparent victory, in the summer of 1999 the situation remained unclear in many aspects, most particularly about the
future status of the province, the longer-term role of military forces
and the stance, both present and future, of Russia.

Here was a test case of several contemporary assertions: that
NATO could have a more generalized role as both a peace enforcer
and then peacekeeper in post-Soviet Europe – and perhaps further
afield; that using force in these circumstances could be antiseptically
achieved from the air, thus both avoiding widespread civilian casualties and casualties to the enforcers; that the doctrines and equipment which NATO had retained from its former role as the deterrent
alliance of the West would be as effective against a mountain civil
war as against the Warsaw Pact; and, on a rather different plane,
that the rights inherent in national sovereignty now took a secondary position to the human rights of a population; that, therefore, a legal war, at least in a customary sense, could be fought and
supported by public opinion to defend those rights where national
interests in a traditional sense were not involved. Moreover, the role
of the UN was called into question in that it would not authorize a
military defence of the Albanians, since some members of the

Security Council were clear that to do so would have been beyond the authority of the Charter, but it also refused to declare such a defence illegal, once it was under way. No final conclusions have emerged at the time of writing, but it is already clear that the hopes attached to antiseptic air attacks have been unfounded in that they did not produce any quick change of policy on the part of Serbia, indeed rather the reverse. This has been due both to the emotional effect on the population and to the limitations imposed on its effectiveness by the felt need only to attack limited targets. This gave the Serb government time to step up its efforts to expel the Albanian majority, who fled to neighbouring countries, thus creating a humanitarian refugee crisis of huge proportions, for which governments both local and distant were plainly unprepared.

It thus seems as if the changing pattern of conflict is not amenable to the tactics believed in and military assets possessed by NATO and that, therefore, if its role is to be changed, its nature and equipment will have to be adapted to match. It also looks very much as if the use of force remains just that, even if its application has not been dictated by traditional national interests. The idea that it was both possible and right that war should be undertaken in a different and less involved way if it was being fought in the interests of human rights seems not to be sustainable. The only way to achieve the return of the Albanian population to their homes in Kosovo has turned out to be escorting them home under military protection on the ground, not just in the air, and, if necessary, expelling the Serb forces as this is done. Furthermore, the returned Albanians will require external support, physical protection and public administration for a long time to come. They will have to form some kind of international protectorate, neither a state nor a province, but a new kind of geopolitical animal.

If all this continues, it will begin to look as if the clock is being turned back. The long parabola which began to unite the practice and incidence of war with contemporary combinations of state power and improving technology had the effect of gradually reducing the incidence of war while steadily increasing its reach when it did happen until the whole of a society was inextricably involved. Wars became fewer but harsher and more destructive. Now it may be that we have arrived at the end of that parabola. The connection between ever more organized state power and war is becoming looser again, opening the way for a much more fluid, more or less ever-present, skein of violence, usually within individual societies, which it is often possible to ignore even when quite close at hand. Standards of human behaviour are declining, not least because the treaties created to control the worst excesses of warfare and captivity depended on reciprocity between state governments rather than legal retribution for their force, to the extent that they do work or have done so. That reciprocity does not exist to the same degree between fighting groups not located in a state structure or in any case engaged in genocide.

There is, however, and finally a more sinister point to note. At the moment when the bipolar international system collapsed, arms development was moving rapidly beyond the nuclear, generally believed to be out of date as well as unusable, into the era of smart weapons and possibly laser weaponry, though they have not yet been successful. Greater and greater precision was the goal. Instead, as has been said, we have more and more rather blunt weapons in use, except in one area. It is cheap and comparatively easy – learnable from the Internet – how to make and release biological and chemical weapons. Poisoning wells and contaminating food supplies was a feature of the Thirty Years War, but it was not very efficiently done and it excited great moral objections – ignored, naturally, by the perpetrators. It is not in the least difficult to see how the mounting chaos of our own time may give both to weakened rulers and small opposing groups the taste for quick and overwhelming victory by using such weapons, and it is the respect in which civilian populations to some degree released from the threat of total war since 1989, are yet facing something potentially equally dreadful. In its uncontrollable and unknowable effects, it may possibly be worse than anything hitherto. What remains of the global state system has to be mobilized to deal with this problem, probably as much by developing antidotes as by attempting to create and police a controlling regime.

3.6 Attempts to secure peace

Contemporary war, as we have seen, has been changed by secondary consequences of globalization as applied to the national state and has begun a new phase of evolution. Attempts to preserve peace will also have to move into a new phase. Indeed, there are now so many gradations of violent conflict that the traditional meanings of the words 'peace' and 'war' can no longer give an accurate account of what is happening. In this they join other casualties already mentioned: for example, the concepts of 'national interest' and 'foreign' policy. The reverse aspect of the willingness to build up the sinews of war and from time to time actually to go to war has been a steadily increasing effort to maintain peace. This has been particularly true since 1815 because from the Vienna settlement onwards, there has been a continuously evolving mechanism for preserving peace between states. Like war, however, making or keeping peace has been closely related to the needs and expectations of states and their governments. In very recent times, again like warfare, that relationship has been broken in important ways by the effects of the globalizing trends we have been discussing. What has negatively affected the scope and stability of national governments generally has also affected their ability and the ability of organizations created by states, to control conflict. In addition, contemporary conflict itself may as often arise from the internal weakness of a state as from any aggressive or expansionary intentions a national government might have. Given that new ways of thinking about how to preserve peace must follow from new understandings about what causes warfare, internal as much as or more than inter-state, we need now to consider how previous such efforts have evolved.

The desirability of peace has never been in doubt, even at historical periods when the distinction between peace and war was a good deal less clear than it has been in recent times. From classical times to Shakespeare we are accustomed to the expression of such emotions: 'Why that naked, poor and mangled Peace, Dear nurse of arts, plenties and joyful births...' (*Henry V*). John Wilkes, on the other hand, ever ready to mock the British government, pilloried the Peace of Paris (1763) – saying 'it must be the Peace of God, for it passeth all understanding' – a rather wicked reference to the formal blessing stipulated in the Book of Common Prayer of the Anglican Church. There have, however, also been times when peace has not seemed better than war. Lord John Russell remarked in 1853, as the Crimean War approached: 'If peace cannot be maintained with honour, it is no longer peace.' This could be felt quite often when warfare was less overwhelming than technological advances in slaughtering devices rendered it towards the end of the nineteenth century, but it has surfaced even since then. While Neville Chamberlain explained, as British Prime Minister in 1938, that 'In war, whichever side may call itself the victor, there are no winners but all are losers', Winston Churchill was writing

> I have watched this island descending incontinently, fecklessly, the stairway which leads to a dark gulf. It is a fine broad stairway at the beginning, but after a bit the carpet ends. A little farther on there are only flagstones, and a little further on still these break beneath your feet.

And when that process had resulted in war, he told an audience of schoolboys 'Do not let us speak of darker days; let us rather speak of sterner days. These are not dark days: these are great days – the greatest days our country has ever lived...' (Harrow School, 1941). Sometimes a particular peace can excite contempt. Immediately after the 1919 settlement was signed in the Hall of Mirrors at Versailles, the French Marshal Foch turned to a neighbour and said 'Peace, Peace – it is not Peace, it is an armistice for 20 years': a chillingly accurate assessment, as it turned out. Humanity has always been as ambiguous about peace as it is about sin.

Pre-Vienna

During the earliest phases of the modern state, warfare was common and in the case of the Thirty Years War, significantly unpleasant. When it ended in 1648 the urge to return to peace was stronger than at any previous time, and the emergence of a structure of international law gave the protection of peace a point of reference over and beyond the sensible conduct of foreign policy. There was bound to be a period of mixed responses, before the emergence of sovereign states was sufficiently complete to place the responsibility for peace and war firmly and solely on the shoulders of rulers and, subsequently, governments. The result was a particularly instructive debate in which lawyers, philosophers and political commentators sought to develop schemes which would reproduce the imagined peaceful relations of an equally imaginary past using means derived from the dog-eat-dog world of the developed and developing sovereign state. These schemes were not successful. They ranged from the naive to the richly comic and they signally failed to appeal to rulers – perhaps unsurprisingly. Little progress was made until the end of the Napoleonic Wars in 1815, when for the first time a fully political rather than purely philosophical attempt was made to preserve peace. The fundamental reasons were that the war had confirmed rather than altered a rough equality between the major states, which meant that none was likely to win any war against another. Secondly, as we have noted earlier in the context of the evolution of political legitimacy, the activity of governance had reached a point of development where going to war, itself a more compelling business than it had formerly been, implied such serious deceleration for internal progress and development that its disruptions were to be avoided as far as possible.

The Congress of Vienna thus behaved very differently from the congresses which preceded the Westphalia settlement in 1648. From an early date – 1805 – two governments at least, the British and the Russian, had agreed that just defeating Napoleon was not enough and that there would have to be a whole new international dispensation to bring order to international relations and prevent any recurrence of the previous conflict. At this stage, they did not face up to the problem – except by appealing to the Public Law of Europe, which was a singularly vague concept – of how in practical terms this effect could be achieved. This is what William Pitt, then Prime Minister of England, wrote to the Tsar of Russia, the quixotic Alexander I, in 1805: the peace treaty, when it came, he said, should not only resettle Europe territorially but also

> reestablish a general and comprehensive system of Public Law in Europe, and provide, as far as possible for repressing future attempts to disturb the general tranquillity, and, above all, for restraining any projects of aggrandizement and ambition similar to those which have produced all the calamities inflicted on Europe since the disastrous era of the French Revolution.

The nearest he came to suggesting how this might be done was to propose a treaty of general guarantee to confirm whatever settlement was made. Later, in March 1814, when the war was plainly nearing its end, the allied powers agreed that special measures by which they would jointly control international relations would be necessary for 20 years after peace was concluded; but there was still no hint of how this would be done. After November 1814, when the final work on the settlement began at Vienna, the idea of a special and extra treaty of guarantee resurfaced and drafts were prepared. The Congress was lengthier than expected, however, and Napoleon made his spectacular escape from Elba and had to be finally defeated all over again and exiled rather further away. During this time, both the English and the Russians retreated from the idea of a special treaty. The English did so because the longer the war was over, the less they liked the idea of undertaking any permanent obligations which might involve military intervention in Europe, for all the same reasons that the Americans were later to refuse to subscribe to the League of Nations covenant.

The Russian Tsar, however, had moved in the opposite direction. He now wanted something much more eccentric and potentially more binding. His views were always powerfully affected by whoever happened to be his mistress and the chosen lady in 1815 was the Baroness Krüdener. She was a deeply devout, if uncomplicated, Christian, and the Tsar decided that a treaty compelling rulers to behave towards each other in a Christian and brotherly fashion would ensure peace in the future. Other rulers were both amused and contemptuous but, with the exception of the British Prince Regent, signed up. The treaty, which had only two clauses, declared in its second that princes had a duty to assist each other; and it was that apparently anodyne statement which was quickly to make the Holy Alliance into a charter for autocratic monarchs resisting revolutionary threats. Whether as an expression of Christian hope or as a justification for intervention against revolutions, the Alliance was doomed to failure, and right up to the end of the final treaty-making in November 1815, there remained a hole where some practical device was required for protecting the future of peaceful international relations.

The hole was eventually filled, at least partly, and the way it was done profoundly affected the whole future of structured, rather than purely emotional, attempts to resolve disputes and preserve peace. In order to understand what happened, it has to be remembered that during the latter stages of the war, a final coalition of allies had to be held together for long enough to defeat Napoleon militarily. It was more likely to be successful because Napoleon was severely weakened following the disaster of his Russian campaign; but it was also more likely to be subject to divisions as the prospect of victory engendered both potential differences among the allies and the chances that Napoleon himself might initiate negotiations for peace. It was this last possibility that triggered a new development of great importance. In the winter and early spring of 1814, following the decision of the British Cabinet to send the Foreign Secretary, Robert Stewart, Lord Castlereagh, to Europe, a small group of allied ministers and the Tsar of Russia coalesced, initially at Basle in Switzerland. The purpose was to deal quickly and unitedly with any proposals that Napoleon might make, for the British particularly important since they were furthest away. In the event he made none, believing that his position would be lost unless he achieved a military victory.

So the war dragged on for four months, until May 1814, when he finally abdicated as the allied forces approached Paris. During that time, the ministers followed the campaign as it moved to and fro, acting as a kind of semi-permanent political directorate for the coalition, defusing crises and maintaining allied unity. The same group dealt with the restoration of the Bourbons in France and made a treaty with Louis XVIII and then began preparing the ground for the forthcoming Congress at Vienna. By this time, their work had been noticed by the smaller powers who resented being excluded from what had effectively become an allied cabinet made up of men who knew each very well and had shared many physical and political hardships and survived them. The group also survived the objections of the smaller powers and when the practicalities of the Congress forced them to accept the participation of Talleyrand, representing France, they had achieved something never before seen: the committee of five (Britain, Austria, Russia, Prussia and France) was not only highly experienced, but also accurately reflected the reality of the distribution of power among the greater states. This was an essential precondition for effective activity.

Post-Vienna: 1815–1919

As it turned out, this basically practical piece of the nuts and bolts of victory and peacemaking was to be the model for future development. For when the hole came to be filled in November 1815, neither ideology nor principle was used, but this already existing standing conference. It was agreed on 20 November 1815 that it should be maintained: the sovereigns or ministers of the great powers would continue to meet at fixed intervals in peacetime – itself previously unheard of – and it was also agreed that their role would be almost unlimited: 'for the purpose of consulting on their common interests, and for the consideration of the measures which at each of these periods shall be considered the most salutary for the repose and prosperity of Nations and for the maintenance of the Peace of Europe'. From that day to the present, there has always been some kind of mechanism for pursuing a cooperative management of international relations, and as the system has developed, it has done so in a direct line of evolution from the first meeting of the allied ministers at Basle in January 1814.

As the Revolutionary and Napoleonic Wars became more remote and the general international context evolved, the new European system modified itself in parallel and as the century progressed became global in scope. The general international situation followed patterns set by a more or less even distribution of power among the greater states which limited the potential threat derived from real or attempted revolutions and, as in the eighteenth century, reduced the incidence of warfare. The dual processes which created ever more advanced and expensive techniques of war and ever more complex and politically fragile systems of government within states, created a marked reluctance on the part of governments to go to war and a strong tendency for them to resort to alternative methods of achieving objectives or countering threats.

The chief beneficiary of this reluctance was the Concert of Europe. Concert in this case had less to do with musical harmony than it did with concerted efforts, and those concerted efforts were directed through a version of the system that was inaugurated in 1815. The great powers had not found it possible to live with the restrictions on their sovereignty that fixed meetings, wielding great power, implied. But they had found that the principle that great powers had both the right and the duty to regulate international relations in a crisis or pre-crisis situation by means of special peacetime conferences to be both acceptable and effective. There was little difficulty if the differences of lesser powers stood to be resolved even if they were clients of greater ones. Among the great powers themselves, differences were much more intractable, and it became clear that while wars within the European system were either fought only under very great pressure or were extremely brief, they could not actually be eradicated. Outside the system, as for example the Crimean War of 1854–56, or wars in the Far East or in the Americas, matters continued in a traditional and frequently bellicose way.

The result of this was that while the conference method was absorbed into the machinery of diplomacy, its novelty largely forgotten, other means seemed to be needed. This was particularly obvious after the American Civil War and the European Wars of Italian and German Unification filled the 1860s with conflicts. The results came in four forms: a new effort to have international law codified and enacted so as to become the recognized instrument of dealing with disputes; secondly, the further elaboration of the principle and techniques of arbitration; thirdly, an attempt at disarmament, this particularly fuelled by the crippling expenditure that ever more technologically advanced armaments imposed on governments; fourthly, rather differently focused, the steady accumulation of new legal restrictions (the Geneva Conventions) on the allowable levels of violence, both on combatants and civilians, accompanied by the first emergence of humanitarian organizations such as the Red Cross. The first was not supported by governments, except in so far as great progress was made in codifying the rules of diplomacy, to the point where the Cambridge Rules, informally promulgated in the 1890s, became an accepted norm. Later, after the League of Nations failed to enact a revised version, the Harvard Rules of the 1930s supplanted them and survived until the ratification of the 1961 Vienna Convention on Diplomatic Relations. Arbitration proved to have more staying power in some areas. Where disputes did not involve the 'vital interests' of great powers and were mainly or wholly administrative in scope, there was a sharp increase in the use of arbitration in the late nineteenth century. Over more 'sovereign' matters, the general reaction was well described by the US delegate – particularly evocative, coming as it did from the representative of a power which tended to regard itself as above and beyond the 'selfish' motives of longer-established nations. 'Not a single power was willing to submit all questions to arbitration – least of all the United States. A few nations were willing to accept it in minor matters. ...'

These matters were in practice more important than the US delegate was willing to admit. They were a consequence of the vast increase in administrative cooperation which advancing technology and advancing government powers together created. Health, transport, postal and telegraphic communications were the chief areas of activity involved and a genuine corpus of international legislation grew up, replete with rights, duties and enforcable penalties; and arbitration, or other legal means, proved to be an acceptable way of resolving the inevitable resulting disputes. The other serious advantage of arbitration was the opportunity it gave to governments, increasingly concerned by the need to remain politically popular, to shelve or postpone issues that might evoke strong nationalist public emotions, forcing a sharp response inimical to the real national interest. This is an important reason why territorial disputes, sometimes even of great powers like the USA and Britain, were quite frequently submitted to arbitration. For smaller powers, particularly in Latin America, the technique was very widely used. This was recognized in 1899 with the establishment of the International Court of Arbitration at The Hague – the beginning of a long story whose most recent manifestation has been the campaign to establish an international criminal court.

The Hague Conference, whose centenary was celebrated in 1999, at least partly represented a response to a sea change in international relations which was rapidly substituting general anxiety for the general security which had come to seem almost pre-ordained since the defeat of Napoleon. How deeply ingrained in the public memory Bonaparte was and for how long peace had largely predominated can be seen from the fact that Sir Edward Grey, British Foreign Secretary 1905–16, recorded that his Nanny used to tell him that if he was not good, 'Boney would come and find him'. It was not surprising that rising anxiety provoked both traditional attempts to buttress national security and defend national interests by creating alliances to deter perceived enemies – itself a shockingly new categorization of a neighbour – and by expanding military forces. It also led to attempts at disarmament, or at least reduction of armaments, and to efforts to avoid surprising military increases by exchange of information. But the advance of the arms race, the fear that the objectives of at least some powers had ceased to be directed at serving national interests by intelligent and intelligible *raison de système*, overwhelmed all attempts to underpin the Concert of Europe. The last meeting of the Concert took place in St James's

Palace, London, during the period September 1912 to May 1913 and its success in controlling a serious Balkan War was a very close-run thing. One year later, it seemed obvious to most powers that it should be recalled to deal with the local Austro-Serbian crisis caused by the assassination of the Archduke Francis Ferdinand at Sarajevo. But the German government refused to allow it to meet, partly because it wanted to support its ally, Austria-Hungary, and partly because its own concerns had passed beyond the issues arising from the murders. An opportunity seemed to offer to resolve both an internal, constitutional crisis and an external panic, chiefly caused by the rising strength of Russia, by means of a well-prepared, anti-septic and brief European war.

The end of the war to end all wars: 1919 and after

The preparations, which were real enough, did not suffice and the war which ensued spiralled rapidly out of control – of the strategists, the tacticians, the politicians and above all the ordinary people, who died in previously unimagined millions. For the last years of the war, and importantly for the Americans who joined late in the day, the slaughter was only justifiable – if then – on the plea that the object of victory was to 'end all wars'. Although this objective overlay other more mundane intentions, there was no doubt that the abolition of war had to be attempted at the peace conference which met at Paris in April 1919. For the ravaged peoples of Europe the idea was quite simple, perhaps simplest where Marxists could equate the coming universal revolution with the end of states and thus of enmities between them. But it was not simple to achieve, not least because it came accompanied by much baggage from the past. Naturally it was asked what had caused the previous war – as it had been in 1814. Then the answer was quite clear: revolution, and the delegates went to work to render it powerless in the future. They also had shared views about the distribution of power and the machinery of international relations. In 1919 neither condition was repeated. The mixture of inherited machinery and opinions about the cause of the war was similar, but the similarity ended there. When people answered the question in 1918, they gave widely differing replies: Germany had caused the war; the arms race and/or the alliance system had caused the war; imperialism had created new tensions; nationalism had been behind the assassinations; the system of conferences had failed; neither arbitration nor any other legal process had been tried. Nor was there agreement about either the basic ideology or the machinery of international relations or the real or preferred distribution of power. The muddle, both intellectual and practical, was on an epic scale. The result was entirely predictable.

The treaty settlement ended up as a smorgasbord of attempts to neutralize most of these dangers. The Treaty of Versailles was designed to emaciate Germany territorially and economically; other treaties attempted to draw the teeth of nationalist aspirations, particularly in Central Europe; disarmament was imposed on Germany with the idea that all others would follow; the beginnings of the end of empires – a particularly American objective – was compassed by removing what had been Germany's. The most important provision, however, was the establishment of the League of Nations. Its Covenant contained all the other dishes of the smorgasbord table. It was partly an institutionalized form of the Concert of Europe. The structure of the League, particularly in the creation of the Council of the League, was designed first and foremost to prevent any repetition of a situation when any one or combination of states could prevent the calling of a conference at a moment of crisis. The contrast between the success – however difficult – of 1912–13 and the catastrophe of 1914 was too recent and too obvious to ignore. Never in the future was it to be possible to evade a conference, for the conference was permanently in existence; nor was the time factor to be allowed to become urgent, as provisions for cooling off were also written in. Moreover, misinformation was to be avoided by special machinery for investigation and report. The failure of diplomacy in 1914 was also to be rectified. The machinery of diplomacy was now to be reinforced, even supplanted, by the machinery of the League, again ineluctable, and, moreover, replete with all the authority which the representatives of elected governments could give it – there were to be no other kinds of government – as opposed to the professional diplomatic services who were deemed, however wrongly, to have failed to prevent war breaking out in 1914. Never again would public opinion be excluded from the making of foreign policy, or free-wheeling diplomacy send peoples to war without their consent. This democratic expression was intended to be the most powerful weapon available to the League, and in the immediately postwar atmosphere it was not conceived that public opinion might be capable of tolerating or even encouraging war at some point in the future. The League was also deliberately equipped with the means to prevent the re-emergence of a network of alliances with secret provisions, unknown to the peoples who were nonetheless committed to fight because of them. The League was further given the oversight of disarmament, the task of codifying international law for the benefit of the new International Court, and the administration of the former German colonies, largely in practice mandated to the British.

By the time the drafters of the Covenant had finished, there were few, perhaps actually no, techniques for preventing war that were not available to the international community through the League. But all these good intentions and richness of opportunities failed. The very complexity of the League system probably militated against it, but, at bottom, it was not the constitution of the League, still less the intentions of its progenitors that were central to its fate, so much as the international circumstances of the time. At its core there was a fundamental flaw: Woodrow Wilson, afforced with all the authority and largely untouched military power of the United States, came all the way across the Atlantic to insist on a complete change in the conduct of international relations. This change which was intended to meet the general aspirations of all people but also the particular emotions and objectives of the United States, succeeded to a remarkable degree, not so much in the provisions of each treaty, though there was much of his distaste for Germany in the Versailles Treaty, but in the terms of the Covenant of the League. This theoretical success remained absolutely dependent for its practical achievement on the presence and commitment of the United States. In fact, the terms of all the treaties were so far removed from the possibility of practical compliance in the real world that only the forcible support of the United States could enforce them against the odds, and Wilson failed to deliver that support. Without it, the League's own method of enforcement was unviable. The contemporary total public rejection of war as an instrument of policy meant that the League could not be equipped with any weapons of military enforcement. The equally contemporary belief in the global supremacy of economic power provided the substitute. It had been strong enough even before 1914 to provoke one famous treatise, arguing that its very existence now prevented governments from going to war because of the economic damage that would inevitably follow. It was beliefs of this kind that lay behind the introduction of economic sanctions as the League's mode of punishment. Sanctions, as we very well know, are exceedingly difficult weapons to use, much subject to the effects of the doctrine of unexpected consequences and liable to be leaky in their application. This last tendency was very marked in the case of the League and made the absence of the USA, the USSR and Germany from its membership highly significant.

The overall result was unappealing. Germany remained the greatest power in Europe, but was debarred from taking any responsibility for its future, having been excluded from the League and placed under specific disadvantages by treaty. Yet her principal restraints had largely been destroyed: Russia, not even a member of the League, vanished into isolation under Lenin and Stalin, France was weakened in every way, the British largely absent and the Habsburg Empire dissolved into a myriad of incompetent yet competing elements. The economic shackles which heavy reparations payments were meant to provide disappeared into endless rescheduling agreements, until they actually vanished altogether. The French, who had lost most, returned to the belief that their security could only be realized by the most traditional of means – armaments and alliances, while the British withdrew into a penurious and querulous defence of their possessions and attempted to reconstruct the sinews of economic power. The chaotic results of the effort to relieve nationalist pressures in Eastern and Central Europe gave every opportunity for self-interested interference from outside; in Asia the continuing weakness of China and the relative success of Japan promised that the restraints of the Washington treaties, naval and political, would be impermanent.

When the Great Depression broke into so fragile and fractious a world, the results were rapidly rapacious. Japan seized Manchuria in 1931, Italy conquered Abyssinia in 1935, Japan began occupying large sectors of China in 1937, Germany acquired Austria in April 1938, a substantial part of Bohemia in September 1938 and all of it in March 1939. In September 1939, just 21 years after the war to end all wars had ended, Germany invaded Poland, smartly joined by the Soviet Union. In 1940, Norway, Holland, Belgium and France were also invaded, to be joined by Italy fresh from attempted invasions in the Balkans and Greece. Finally in 1941, first in the summer with the German invasion of the Soviet Union and then in December with the Japanese attack on Pearl Harbor, followed by Hitler's declaration of war on the United States, a conflict on a global scale began. Nothing further from the promise of the 1919 settlement and the League of Nations – whom no one bothered to inform of the outbreak of war in 1939 – could have been imagined. Except on the Soviet–German front, the horrific slaughter of the First World War was not repeated. But the war had involved civilians to an unheard-of degree, had covered a geographical area of huge size and had ended with nuclear bombardment of the Japanese. The whole war effort dominated every aspect of life – private, public, economic and political, and because of the perceived connection between fascism, bellicosity and genocide, its end was seen to be an ideological triumph – either for liberal democracy or communism. When it ended, a new attempt to prevent its repetition was bound to be made and once again the attempt was powerfully influenced by the structures of the past and contemporary views as to what had caused the war.

The United Nations and the contemporary world

The structures of the past – chiefly the League of Nations – were rebuilt in the light of the perceived causes of the war just ended. This time the answers were naturally different. The war had been caused by aggressive fascist regimes propelled partly at least by the economic failure of the Depression. Thus great efforts were made to defend economic stability through the establishment of new supranational economic and financial institutions. The failure of the League was seen to have been caused by flaws in its constitution, particularly its respect for the complete sovereign independence of its members as expressed through the unanimity rule and by the absence of important states – particularly the USA. A new organization, the United Nations, was constructed, which the United States was careful to join and which reflected in its Charter the general belief that the League had been too weak. The Charter of the UN gave additional powers to the Security Council – the successor to the Council of the League – as a result of a deal by which the most powerful states were induced to accept the existence of this extra authority in exchange for not being themselves subject to it. They became permanent members of the Security Council, a kind of managing committee and thus responsible for balancing the commitment of the UN organization to maintaining the sovereignty of member states with the new obligation to breach that sovereignty in certain circumstances. Those circumstances revealed another lesson learnt from recent history. The provisions of the Covenant had started from the assumption that many wars started from disputes that ran out of control. Thus the machinery of the League must make that impossible, which it indeed tried to do. The makers of the Charter, having experienced Hitler, Mussolini and the Japanese, did not think that disputes ran out of control: they knew they could be deliberately pushed.

Thus the emphasis in the Covenant on dealing with disputes changed in the Charter to an emphasis on dealing with episodes of aggression. In such events, the Security Council, given the agreement of the permanent members, was handed very broad powers, far broader than anything the League had possessed. In addition, it was widely thought that the League's failure was partly due to its lack of military power and its reliance solely on the weapon of economic sanctions. The latter weapon was retained by the UN and is, of course, in current use, but it was also intended to equip the new organization with military forces; and in the early stages a curious competition developed between the USSR and the USA as to who could suggest the largest military establishment to be allocated. In the event none was or has ever been, for the same reason that the permanent members did not establish themselves as a world managing committee or an international cabinet. External circumstances, very different in each case, undermined the function of the international organization charged with keeping peace. In the case of the League, war rapidly ensued; in the case of the UN, few wars ensued and none between the major powers. But in both cases, the organization was essentially ignored, except for propaganda purposes, whether it was the exit of the Japanese in 1932, or the drama of Mr Khruschev's (specially imported) shoe used to bang the table in 1961.

One serious difference remains for discussion. The Cold War stalemate preserved the UN in aspic. Unlike the League it did not disappear into a maelstrom of conflict. It met other needs – those of developing states, for example, for a time – but at the end of the

Cold War, there it was, looking around hopefully like a baby dinosaur newly discovered in a hitherto unknown part of the jungle. The immediate response was to offer it bananas, or at least the prospect of bananas. It would be the chief agency of the New World Order, maybe it would now get access to military forces; the powers of the Security Council, even its membership, would be changed and improved. A few years on, this all seems utterly improbable. Little has changed in the UN's relations with its members, though, internally, there have been some reforms. Why should this be so? It is scarcely as if there is less conflict since the end of the bipolar era or less need of skilled cooperative management of global affairs.

To understand this, we have to remember that the same globalizing changes that helped to bring about the end of the bipolar regime have also brought about a change in the causes of conflict and thus what is required to preserve peace. The Concert of Europe could not cope with a global international system or with serious imbalance in the distribution of power. The League could not cope with governments who did not just want their legal rights endorsed in a generally stable world, but wished instead to improve their political circumstances by force if necessary. The UN cannot deal with a world in which it is not so much the dangers of bellicose relations between member states which have to regulated, as the consequences of civil or nationalist strife within member states, followed in a steady stream by their collapse. Nothing in the Charter or its subsequent evolution offers much that is helpful in these circumstances and the roll call of UN failures has become a commonplace of anti-UN expression, particularly by those who do not yet understand why the failures have occurred. The UN was set up by governments to deal with governments on a bilateral or occasionally multilateral basis. Only very recently, in connection with humanitarian operations, environmental and human rights issues, has it begun to deal with entities who are not governments. These contacts have been noticeably more successful than those with states, and since no way has yet been found to relieve the causes of internal violence and state collapses, it is in relieving the symptoms that the most good can be done. It may be the case – a very long shot – that in evolving towards this function and away from the mechanisms of neutralizing inter-state conflict, a way will be found to move to the eradication of the fundamental causes of this kind of conflict. But, if so, it will not be by the evolution of the UN alone. It remains the world's principal antidote to war and its principal guardian of peace, but it was recognized in the early days that the world's financial system and its economic development also required management. Governments set up inter-governmental institutions to do this – the IMF, the World Bank and GATT, now the WTO, in particular. As we have seen earlier, they, too, operate essentially on a basis that expects governments to be in control of their local economic and financial circumstances and thus able to enter into agreements that will introduce outside help, sometimes in return for domestic policy changes. How these interventions work powerfully affects how much internal conflict there may be at a moment when such conflict has moved to centre stage. Yet these organizations are committed to dealing with governments whose hold on life is at best tenuous and whose position may actually be terminal. They are in any case simply not able to have dealings, even where that is itself a practical possibility, with the causes and causers – for example currency speculators – of the economic and social crises which need to be relieved.

It is thus one of the great contemporary ironies that all the accumulated experience of three centuries and more of what causes war and all the consequential suffering is now becoming irrelevant. The kinds of wars that states, rulers and governments embarked on or defended themselves against are becoming less common and less likely, and whole elaborate systems of technologically highly advanced weaponry are left rotting and apparently purposeless as a result. Yet we face major breakdowns of ordinary peaceful existence, atrocities casually committed on a scale that we find difficult to comprehend and whole complex webs of economic and trading relationships destroyed. Much conflict is conducted by small groups, sometimes more in the character of bandits, acting for sub-state entities, and it is not easy for the organized armies inherited from the Cold War world to react successfully to them. This leads to a difficult problem about the one remaining major military alliance: NATO. The purpose for which it was constructed, supported over a long period and steadily modified, has largely evaporated; however during the crisis over the human rights of the Albanian population of the Kosovo province of Serbia in 1998–99, an attempt was made to use it, as antiseptically as possible, to enforce the human rights of the Albanians at the expense of the sovereign rights of Serbia. The final results are not known at the time of writing, but the attempt has plainly not been successful in the way intended, and the whole affair has reinforced the notion that the patterns of conflict, the rights of states, the obligations of the global community towards people have all been changed profoundly. With that change comes inevitable concomitant change in the role of alliances, military and non-military, and that of the United Nations. All are in a transitional state, not just the usual steady modification that the passage of time imposes, but structural change induced by a wholly new global political and economic environment.

This is why the causes of these events do not lie where we are accustomed to look and they cannot be prevented by the leaders we have either elected or otherwise acquired. Failure of leadership is not the cause of contemporary conflict, for it is not amenable to such leaders and they increasingly engage less and less public interest and support as a result. For the truly visionary, a new start must be made in which the causes of the oppression and injustice which lead to warfare, and which are unlikely to lie in any individual human behaviour, are clearly identified and given some form which makes them at least as subject to pressure as any government once was and hopefully more so. Perhaps we need to learn more about attitudes to peace in the pre-state era instead of trying to accommo-date their contemporary fallibility. Certainly, before ambassadors came to represent only states and many entities claimed to be able to and actually did represent themselves, there was a general view that diplomacy had a general function of preserving peace. Listen to Ambassador du Rosier writing in 1436: 'The business of an ambas-sador ... is peace. ... An ambassador is sacred because he labours for the general welfare.' Unless we can do this and more, we, too, in our different ways, will be trying as the League did, to prevent disputes from running out of control, when that is not what they now do, or, like the IMF, trying to negotiate unfulfillable conditions from a gov-ernment which did not cause and cannot influence the troubles of its people. What is actually required is some globally operating mechanism for stopping civil conflict and applying administrative and financial rescue packages as needed. It is improbable that national governments will be able to do this by combining – all experience is against the notion – so a highly plural entity that operates horizontally, disconnected from vertical structures, however they might be conjoined, will have to be conjured into existence if any progress is to be made. The lesson is the same here as elsewhere in this discussion: what constitutes power and where it is located have to be accurately identified and then equipped with controlling mechanisms and conscripted into the business of restraining violent conflict, willingly conscripted because of the obvious advantages of doing so. Attempts to achieve this based on expecting to find all real power located in states or associations of states will simply not work.

4
Conclusion

It is gradually becoming possible to discern through the mist what this is leading to, as well as what it is caused by. The shift to horizontally arranged areas of activity rather than vertically constructed centres of power is evoking a response in much the same way as the emergence of states did two and a half centuries ago. States, their internal structure and their external associations, have been the principal losers and human activities of every sort – good and bad – have been the beneficiaries. In some of these activities, pressure can be detected in rising anxieties about management and control – even demands for it – without yet having yielded any hard consequences: the easy availability of potentially damaging information and techniques via the Internet is an example of this. Some organizations, generally not connected with or originating from national governments, have also been beneficiaries. Global companies, quickly modifying themselves to take advantage of new opportunities, are one example. The emergence of globally operating private humanitarian organizations is another. Here, the consequences of their vastly enhanced role in international crises caused by the collapse of states – such as Bosnia or Rwanda – are already taking administrative and representative form such that they exist side by side with the older forms of state-based entities, for example, the United Nations. The result of this is a steadily unfolding shift of emphasis in the most traditional stronghold of state-centred relationships – the sole ownership and use of the machinery of international diplomacy by governments or bodies certified by governments.

The heady mixture of entities all having some kind of role at one level or another in the process of global relations makes up the international environment in which we live: some are rising, some declining. Old rules and familiar practices are decaying, while new ones are being tested. Nor is this merely the result of a sharp rise in the number of entities involved in the global system, however powerful a factor it is. The presence of a strikingly larger number of states operating at very different levels of power and sophistication undoubtedly creates complications. The rising number and importance of private organizations do the same. The transnational global economy brings larger numbers of transnational companies, both creating a larger global commerce and increasing their share of it. All this would create a new global economic and political context and many anxieties and uncertainties on its own. But it is not on its own. The increasing quantity has not just produced new kids on the block: the block itself has changed shape.

The present period is, more than most, markedly pluralistic in the structures and mechanisms by which its affairs are conducted. Important activities of government remain, with systems arranged vertically within states that used to do more, but which still do enough, in some cases actually acquiring different responsibilities, to avoid actual extinction. Remaining also from the past web of relationships between states and their governments are a range of international organizations created by states which share in the decline of their members, but which, like their members, still do enough to justify survival or are capable of adequate adaptation. Even if these justifications were not so, the sheer weight of historical expectations and the force of inertia would keep their motors at least idling for some time yet. So the landscape has important, if somewhat rundown, structures in it which play a part and have to be made to work alongside newer modes of organizing human activities. These occur globally and have the expectable horizontal rather than vertical shape. They seep like a gently rising inundation across and around those physical facts, structures and ideas which are territorially located – like night and day – or carry out territorially based administration and jurisdiction. That is why, just to take one example, it is proving so hard to find the right mix of horizontal and vertical detection, jurisdiction and penalty with which to cope with the rising and dangerous effects of transnational crime on individual human beings, as well as their local systems of governance. It is a good example for another reason: more clearly than in other areas of activity which are similarly affected, it is impossible to describe any part of the activity in any place or country as 'foreign'; everywhere it is in fact domestic in its consequences. Transnational crime has penetrated the foundations of the familiar structures of administration and control and it erodes them as seepage will always do. In this it is a particularly comprehensible example of a general condition: the mounting significance of the Internet and all the related elements of the global information system, as well as electronic commerce, global markets and global companies – in short, the whole panoply of global capitalism.

Some conclusions at least are very clear. Human global society is having to develop a new way of accommodating both upright and flattened mechanisms of economic and political management. At the same time, both the global and the local dimension of human activities and loyalties have to be meshed into a balanced set of interconnected responsibilities. The two together have to be helped to generate acceptable means by which human beings can give their consent to power being exercised in new ways and arrive at a common understanding in broad terms of what the moral basis is from which economic, administrative and political decisions will have their starting point. Perhaps there is a useful analogy in the fate of the great rail stations of the United States. The grand union stations constructed in many cities at the apex of the economic and political power of the big railroads were a representation of their status as much as they were a convenience for travellers. Time passed and so did the railroad passengers. In most cases, not all, as the destruction of the old Pennsylvania Station in New York City demonstrated, the structures remained unused and semi-ruined. But their old single use has now been supplanted by a wholly different multi-use. Restored to grandeur, the rail operation either abandoned or confined to a small role, they have become flagship malls, monuments to global consumerism. They demonstrate that it is possible to adapt structures, to put new wine into old bottles and that they need not be broken. A similar process has turned the great Christian cathedrals of Western Europe into religious museums, temples for the modern global tourist. None of this adjustment is going to be easy. It was a prolonged, difficult and occasionally violent process when the last great evolution produced sovereign states and the states system.

Thus there can be no immediately reassuring things to say about the general situation that we have been exploring. Attempts by politicians to develop them are one of the reasons why electorates believe them less and less. The contemporary world confronts not just the onset but the secondary stages of a general change of direction, the equal and perhaps even more compelling than those that accompanied the fall of the Roman Empire, successive collapses of Chinese dynasties or the Renaissance and Reformation period in Europe. It is certain that new accommodations to new circumstances will be arrived at; they always are. It is at least likely that these accommodations will arise in an evolutionary way in response to needs and events and that attempts either to redirect the flow of events or to resist them are likely to fail and fail in violent circumstances. There are already signs – welcome signs – that new areas of power and activity are beginning to self-generate initial systems of management and control. However, there are no signs yet that the appearance of these new structures are being related either to traditional methods of ensuring that their operations have democratic consent or acquiring new constitutional arrangements of their own. This gap is likely to be the stuff of political conflict and dispute in the immediate future and it contains within it a serious risk of mounting violence. It is quite certainly the most urgent item on the global political agenda.

We have at least two things we can do in the face of all this. The agent of all these changes has been, as we have frequently reminded ourselves, a communications revolution. That revolution has given us universally available information – admittedly a serious overload of it; and we can all, across the globe, get a sense of what is happening and thus be able to understand, even if we do not approve or are personally disadvantaged by, the flow of events. Human beings, whether or not organized in societies governed by states, have, after periods of discomfort and confusion, arrived at a fairly clear-eyed view of what kinds of organizations and behaviour conveyed the best overall advantage, even if that meant kicking over some significant traces to get there. The broadest possible dissemination of information and comprehension of what is happening to us all is the best that we can strive for and the most likely to allow us to enter a very differently constructed world society with the minimum of distress.

The second thing we can do is to ask ourselves, thinking back over the discussion in this book: what are the implications for the structures of governance generally? For national governments the needs are both structural and political. The institutional structures of the state have to be modified so that they are perceived to be doing the job that national governments now must do in an effective way. That job is to maintain the public peace, organize the context of everyday life at the local level and provide for education. It is also to arrange the local economic environment so that the maximum advantage can be reaped, particularly in terms of employment, from global flows of investment. Thus it is additionally the job of national governments to arrange the representation of the state, in common with all others, where decisions are made which alter or change the pace of global developments. Such developments are likely to be economic, financial, environmental, medical or military, and they will impact on each other. And because they are global in scope and operate across states rather than between them, they will be both internal and external at the same time. In structural terms, this means altering national administrative systems so that none has singular responsibility for policy in any one area, since the impact is general, and all can cooperate at all levels. The familiar arrangement of essentially single subject ministries or departments is already breaking down, though the weight of tradition makes it a slow process. In Europe, the British government of the late 1990s was already talking about what it termed 'joined up government' in response to this need, and in doing so was showing signs of wanting to make a closer relationship between what government could actually effectively do and the machinery for doing it.

But reconstructing government administration on the basis of a clear-eyed assessment of its remaining and new responsibilities has to go further. Governments have naturally always taken account of the views and needs of non-governmental actors within their societies, but have generally done so and still may do so, from the commanding heights of the administrative system. This is no longer effective, particularly in the context of the globalized economy and the flows of global investment. Policy and decisions required to implement a government's duty to achieve the best possible economic environment in which to realize the most favourable relationship with the global economy can only be arrived at through a complex mix of private and public, global, central and local authorities. Compared with the past, a heavily diluted, that is inclusive, system of economic management will need to be instituted and many formerly distinct lines and boundaries between public and private will become blurred.

The only way of achieving an appropriate administrative structure will be to reassess what it is that governments are expected to do. It will have to be assessed from the bottom up rather than by reviewing existing functions from the top down. Thus the question as to how, say, a foreign ministry might be reformed so that it functions better in the contemporary global environment tends to lead to a discussion about what different things the existing machinery should be asked to do, perhaps also what it no longer should be asked to do. The proper question to ask concerns what relationships are required with other entities and then try to plan how best to manage them. In the same way, asking what the economic responsibilities of a government are and how they relate to other entities is required before deciding how to fulfil them; similarly with social and environmental issues. What emerges when basic requirements are discussed in this way is usually that the administrative system must be constructed more as a flat plate than as part of a rising pyramid. Managing economic affairs has to bring together private and public employees, a broad range of specialisms in, among other things, environmental science, transport infrastructure and direct links to outside bodies both private – global companies, for example – and public, like trading associations such as the EU or Mercosur, as regionally appropriate. Such an area of operation will find itself operating in company with others, for example one that sets taxation policy or deals with law and criminal justice. Each plate will overlap with others and will have to be able to interact with them where the overlap occurs and to do so at the same level, without travelling up one pyramid to the top and then down inside another one to find an appropriate interconnection, and then, having done so, travel all the way back again armed with the required information or decision. Environmental matters are an example where it is easy to see that these interconnections are bound to exist with economic policy, taxation policy, zoning and physical planning policy, agricultural policy and ultimately legal and criminal justice policies, as well as with entities outside the area of authority of the government in question.

Plainly there are many vested interests involved who would be likely to resist such a major reconstruction of the structure of government, not least the most energetic politicians with ambitions to become secretaries of state and ministers, whose potential fiefdoms would be razed, if not to the ground, to a much lower level of individual significance by such changes. On the other hand power, like water, finds its own level, and failure to adjust will increasingly leave structures with a physical presence but little power and carry the risk that power will move to new positions with little physical structure but much practical authority, a thought which should be anathema to those with the ambition to harness that power to their own careers and advantage. Another great bridge to be crossed is the loss of state sovereignty that is implicit in the fact that internal plates of responsibility will have direct links to external bodies. Of course, there have always been many practical limitations to the idea of complete sovereignty, and since the nineteenth century states have willingly accepted some of these limitations where administrative convenience has been involved – internationally agreed rules for posts and telecommunications, for example. Others have arisen out of such harsh facts, as the influence that very powerful states have had over smaller neighbours. There have always been some objectors to even these facts, but the contemporary situation goes further than any of these, to the point where some people believe that it is only by fully accepting and incorporating a global web of influences and opportunities as well as accommodating objectionable pressures that states can continue to offer a sensible rationale for existence at all. In general, it is usually better to plan for what is going to happen anyway, as it is better to avoid claiming or threatening to do what cannot be done – a point of view frequently and unsuccessfully put by the British Queen Victoria to her ever-active minister, Lord Palmerston.

Part of the outcome of these changes will be determined by the squeeze which the effects of globalization are putting on medium-sized, hitherto unitary, states. There is a clearly visible tendency for societies to give their political allegiance to smaller units, and where this happens it means the construction of larger administrations at local or provincial levels, perhaps to be called states in the future, with corresponding reductions at what had been the central administration. The process works similarly at the other end of the graph. Where large-scale authorities develop, for example, regional economic organizations or global market places, they draw authority away from national governments, who will have to be reduced to match, but require administrative machinery themselves. The need for inclusivity and the blurring of distinctions between public and private will remain the same.

Up to this point, it has been almost entirely downsizing and remoulding government machinery that has been discussed. But the need for newly significant areas of power, particularly economic power, to develop corresponding structures introduces a new element. One of the problems in managing the global economic and financial system is that it lacks machinery with which to do it. Of course it is possible to point to the existence of the IMF, the WTO and the World Bank and it is equally possible to point to possible reforms that might be instituted in them. Even reformed, however, they would remain institutions established in the past and against a very different economic background – one which was substantially controlled by the actions of state governments. The new construction that is required is not to represent the interests of national governments however generalized, but the actual practical existence of the power of global markets. A process has begun, but not yet proceeded very far. It is, however, the only kind of process that is likely to succeed in the end. It is the progression from convenience, in this case the essential convenience of avoiding or at least restraining volatility in global markets, to the point where what is convenient sufficiently establishes itself so that it becomes customary and follows that by generating a structural existence.

The emergence of a formal structure empowered to manage the general affairs and stability of the global markets will then make it possible for it to appoint representatives through whom it can talk to and negotiate with other sources of power and authority, most probably struggle with them and eventually come to mutually satisfactory arrangements. That is how all human institutions which have achieved long-term viability have evolved. It is particularly important that this process speeds up, since the world at present is suffering serious economic disruptions, significantly in Asia, with actual and potential political disorder following, as a result of its inadequacy, if not quite absence. If the gap between the emergence of a source of power and the development of machinery for managing it goes on for too long, highly damaging chaos will supervene. Such chaos is in no one's interest – neither markets, nor national governments nor individual human beings. It therefore needs to be high on the agenda of global economic and financial organizations, national governments and, above all, the markets themselves. The global economy, to borrow a famous phrase, is, like war, too serious a business to be left to the generals. And until all the important parties have evolved suitable machinery for talking to and cooperating with each other, it will be war.

The reorganization of the machinery of government and the acquisition of machinery for managing global sources of power and information will create the possibility of a new global order, arranged horizontally and giving an accurate reflection of the realities of power and authority. If, however, it is merely left at that, it will bequeath a further significant problem. The problem is that of political legitimacy, of how to make a new global order acceptable to human beings, so that they can feel loyalty to it and allow it to exercise authority on their behalf. The means of doing this in respect of the traditional nation state took the form of limiting the untrammelled power, first of rulers, then of executive branches, whether cabinets or presidents and insisting that their role was to achieve the most efficient government possible in whatever were the contemporary terms. In most cases, representative democracy became the chosen means, enshrined in law and constitutions, if in some cases observed less than perfectly. Democracy is felt to be insufficiently installed in the EU, and in respect of such controlling agencies as exist over the Internet or global markets, it has so far found no place. It may be that even with all the global communications to hand, which already allow all sorts of electronic voting techniques – a visit to CNN's site will demonstrate this at once – familiar democratic methods will nevertheless not be able to be transplanted: they were a response to the emergence of sovereign states and may be no more appropriate to the contemporary situation than are other appurtenances of the sovereign state whose reform or demise we have been discussing. There is therefore an urgent necessity to discuss how to gain public acquiescence to global authorities without necessarily either using or replicating methods derived from the experience of the state. Neither the state nor democracy have always existed; but the need for some kind of control on the exercise of power and the sense that it is being exercised in the interests of a population have been generally constant and universal. It is those two considerations from which the making of a new global order acceptable in human terms must start; and it has to be understood that its outcome may not look much like democracy as we have come to know it.

The areas so far discussed have included the future of state government and some areas of global government. We have not yet touched on the management of security, of peace and war and the various possible conditions that lie in between. Here, as in other areas, we face a familiar situation. There exist states and the mechanisms that they have developed – chiefly foreign ministries – for administering what were regarded as external affairs. There also exist entities which are associations of states of one kind or another: the UN is the most comprehensive example, but NATO is another, as, in a very different way, is the EU. To join the club, there have now arrived powerful private organizations, arranged on a global basis and having global constituencies. They chiefly consist of humanitarian, human rights and environmental agencies. They are not new in themselves, but they have changed their roles very significantly and very recently to the point where they represent a new strand in the fabric of global politics. The principal reasons are two: in the case of environmental organizations, it is the coming of global climatic change which has given them a global role, to add to the more specific ones which they have pursued in the past in respect of particularly threatened habitats and flora and fauna. In the case of the other agencies, it is the contemporary tendency for conflict to arise out of state collapses and the apparent ineffectiveness of existing inter-state organizations to cope with the consequences which has made the difference. From acting, usually with amateur and temporary staff, to relieve the immediate effects of natural disasters, or, less often, warfare, these organizations are now finding themselves the chief providers of the services of a state government where none any longer exists and thus facing long-haul and highly complex operations for which more or less permanent and professional staff are required. They can find themselves acting as the equals of state governments, warlords and UN agencies in such situations.

The fundamental cause of this is a change in the pattern of warfare. Wars between states have become very rare, so rare that long periods pass without one occurring. By contrast in 1999, there were 24 civil wars in progress, and many other examples of civil disorder short of actual civil war, as against probably only two traditional inter-state wars. There has also been a change in the character of warfare. The extreme high-tech complexity of the weapons and delivery systems of the Cold War era have given way to low-tech fighting, often more akin to banditry. Meanwhile, the threat of post-modern terrorism, featuring atrocities levelled at masses of innocent civilians, haunts contemporary societies with urban centres. Most of the mechanisms in existence designed to restrain conflict were constructed to restrain inter-state warfare and they do not work well, or sometimes at all, in contemporary circumstances. The contrast between the success of the UN's response to an inter-state war between Iraq and Kuwait, which was a traditional-style invasion, and its ineffectiveness in the internal conflicts in Rwanda or former Yugoslavia demonstrates the point. The hole left by this situation is the one that private organizations have been, often quite reluctantly, filling.

The challenge that the world now faces is to organize its responses differently. This means reforming existing organizations or possibly creating new ones. In the case of the UN, there is a clear division between that part of the organization which has been reacting effectively to the new situation, sometimes by straining the terms of the Charter. This is where the UN has begun to allow formal relationships to develop with private organizations so that they can begin to form part of the system on the one hand, and on the other the UN can influence internal crises through their operations. This practical and increasingly effective response has not yet spread to the more purely political side of the UN's structure – the Security Council, particularly, and the General Assembly. The requirement to respect the sovereignty – at least for most of the time – of member states, and to deal only with the governments of member states has stultified the procedures of the Security Council quite as much as the vetoes of the Cold War years did. This aspect of the UN when held up against the grim realities of world conflict looks like a gap between intentions and means that resembles ships passing in the night. It is obvious that either a reformed UN or a new organization is needed in which membership is extended beyond states and its constitution is constructed so as to reflect horizontal global responsibilities rather than the umpiring of disputes between vertically arranged national governments. The membership of such a new global security authority would include states, humanitarian and human rights agencies, environmental agencies and economic authorities. This last category is required because the connection between growing instability in some states and their loss of major economic decision-making power is clear enough and the role of economic management and global investment flows so significant for civil peace and security that the representatives of both markets and global associations of states have to be included.

Rethinking the membership of a global security authority would be combined with rethinking what its remit and powers should be. Plainly there are three outstanding sources of global insecurity: civil and other conflict, environmental disaster/climatic change and economic inequality or collapse. Power to intervene and enforce in all three areas will have to be given, despite all the potential obstacles which this implies for traditional notions of state sovereignty. Here has to be considered the responsibility for pursuing and apprehending transnational criminals, particularly after crimes of war and genocide have been committed. World opinion has become much more concerned about such issues, and as the war over Kosovo beginning in 1999 confirmed, it has become prepared to resist them by force even when no traditional national interest may be involved. To achieve such enforcement, and to achieve it much earlier in a developing crisis, before full-scale war becomes an issue, some kind of global constabulary will have to be formed to be recruited, managed and used by the global security authority, both in resisting civil strife and maintaining the rule of global law. Because of the changing pattern of conflict, it will be more appropriate to think in terms of a powerful police force rather than an army, an internal rather than an external analogy. In these tactical and strategic terms, it is clear that contemporary conditions have rendered the kind of military doctrines and type of equipment typical of NATO less effective than they were in acting as a deterrent during the Cold War, and a powerful police force would represent a better match between the likely circumstances of conflict, if caught early enough, and an available response to it than a more traditional regional alliance.

Where non-forceful means of enforcement would be desirable, for example, in respect of responsibilities for managing global markets, it will not be sufficient to rely on the weapon of sanctions. The basic notion of isolating a particular territory from the global economy and thereby making it suffer has always had unintended consequences for those not meant to be sanctioned and has not very often been successful in itself. The emergence of a fully global economy makes the notion even more fragile, and late twentieth-century experience with Serbia, Iraq and Cuba underlines the point. It is far more likely that an ability to interrupt the flow of inward investment to a particular area would be more effective, though only on a short-term basis. But even this would be likely to have limited success. Any sustained attempt to prevent work being done at the point where it is both cheap and convenient to do it will in the end be circumvented by some means and to some degree. It is probable that the effects of economic and financial globalization have rendered economic weapons unviable.

It is inevitable that at all times there will be some unanswerable questions. It is particularly difficult at times when public affairs are more than usually transitional, which is evidently true at the turn of this millennium. The kind of world whose make-up and background we have been discussing is composed of the very old, the familiar and traditional mixed with newly minted elements. In some areas the new has ravaged the traditional and thus released the very old: this can be seen in the resurrection of ancient loyalties, the return to distinctly local preoccupations, as it can in some characteristics of contemporary conflict. It is rather as if a long-laid paving stone has been lifted and a whole mini-world of unexpected – and not always attractive – life is suddenly revealed. But in parallel there flows the tide of global communication and activities. The effects of this are highly plastic, largely uncontrolled and so far uncontrollable, but they are beginning to give a certain shape to the world and they are beginning to do more than just weaken or change what was already there. Some institutional structures are beginning to emerge, evolving in response to need and part of the uncertainties and helplessness that can be felt in the face of impersonal and global pressure is attributable to the fact that this process is still at an early stage, only working fitfully and sometimes not at all: its further evolution and refinement are going to be the most important development of the early years of the next millennium and will determine whether human beings reap advantage or disaster from the extraordinary speed and complexity of contemporary technological change.

These developments have changed but not abolished the familiar institutions, political, economic and international which were constructed from the mid-nineteenth century onwards. For a long time to come, world governance will be conducted through a mixed, plural system using both entirely new concepts and entities as well as modified versions of the pre-existing order. Daily life, its opportunities and obligations, will be lived under the management of a system exhibiting contradictory modes of operating, vertical and horizontal, for example, or expressions of authority arranged geographically set against polities which are related to particular activities or interests, having no specific geographical location. Sometimes these will conflict, sometimes combine, sometimes simply fail to connect at all. The process of making a coherent whole out of these differing modes will be the next major task of world political activity. The two most important and difficult aspects will be, on the one hand, to help the institutions which have to fill a lesser role reach that role as peaceably as possible and on the other to insist that those activities which have been pushed by events into prominence and authority should match their power with accessible means of setting limits to it.

In all this, we are approaching what is fundamentally a moral issue and it is most clearly exposed when the future governance of global capitalism and world markets is considered. It is clear that global capitalism has arrived, is persistently and rapidly increasing in its importance but is not universal. It has benefits and costs and is thus both embraced and resisted. The benefits include greater specialization, stronger flows of trade and investment, rapid innovation and greater diffusion of intellectual capital, growth in GNPs, more competition and entrepreneurship and some examples of devolved economic decision taking. The costs are mainly social rather than economic, though both exist. They include transnational market failures, more pronounced economic shocks and volatilities, widening gaps in income distribution, both by area and by type, for example between skilled and unskilled workers, geographical areas excluded from the benefits of globalization and threats to systems of social insurance. Globalization has also made it more difficult to control actual disbenefits – crime, terrorism, illegal immigration and environmental pollution – and has simultaneously reduced the authority of the national governments who largely remain the instruments of regulation.

Despite this powerful list, things have gone too far for resistance to be successful, if it ever could have been, and the effects of resistance are therefore likely to be damaging in every sense without being ultimately successful. This situation makes it urgent to increase the actual and perceived benefits and to reduce the effect of the costs. Only then will it create sustainable wealth and gain broad social acceptance. In order to achieve this, the hitherto disparate working parts of the machinery of global capitalism have to be brought into a coherent and coordinated relationship. These are global markets, national and subnational governments, civil society – in this case, trading associations, non-profit associations, interest groups, clubs – and supranational entities. We have observed already that in addition to the problems inevitably involved in deciding on more or less precise relationships between these parts, some of them lack the means to join in any coordinating exercise because they have yet to develop any representative capacity. Assuming that such a capacity is generated as a response to an evident need, and that mechanisms of coordination do emerge, there will still remain a potentially even more awkward question to be answered.

What will the fundamental moral basis underpinning this new global system be? Past successful economies have had strong moral foundations which emphasized certain moral virtues and discouraged certain dis-virtues and reworkings of the moral bases of societies have preceded new social and economic orders. Beyond the more or less absolute virtues of truth and honesty lie a wide variety of attributes, which may or may not be considered virtues in different cultures, different places and different times. In the present situation, the effect of the global revolution in communications has been to bring these different conceptions of virtues into immediate contact with each other. These cultural collisions are joined by the moral inconsistencies visible in global capitalism itself: the stress on individuality may conflict with the idea of the importance of community, the urge towards wealth creation may not sit comfortably with the maintenance of social justice, the instinct to preserve may be incompatible with the creation of assets. On the other hand there is an impressive list of moral virtues which seem to arise naturally from the chief characteristics of a globalized economy. The significance of intellectual capital and creativity demands imagination, initiative, willingness to learn and relearn continuously, self-discipline, self-confidence and self-respect. The rising significance of cooperation both within and between firms asks for trust, reciprocity, the ability to compromise, adaptability, group loyalty, a sense of the common good and respect for others. The global geography of economic activity evokes a need for an awareness of others, particularly when they are not only different in experience and culture, but also less well off, which leads to neighbourliness, stewardship and a sense of fairness and justice. Without these, working together becomes ineffective.

The question is whether these qualities can form a code which is globally acceptable to the point where it can subsume cultural differences, particularly perhaps 'Asian' values, and reconcile the contradictions inherent in global capitalism. If they can be made to work in this way, then the basic precepts on which the different elements of the global economic system base their coordinative activities will be settled. None need be seen to have trumped another and the essential practical goals which must be reached will have achieved a common point of origin. These goals involve making the regime of global capitalism acceptable by results since it is hard to see how it can be made so by any familiar political processes: thus the propagating of a sense of economic fairness rises to the surface as the most crucial element. The relative weight of responsibility is plainly going to differ. Maintaining adequate social protection within societies for whom globalization brings persistent unemployment will fall to national governments. Providing protection from exploitation where it brings an explosion of low-paid work will fall to both national governments and employers, whether they are local or global or both. Paying attention to the social consequences of schemes of economic and financial restructuring, such as occurred in Indonesia and Thailand in the late 1990s, will have to become part of the calculations of supranational bodies and the yet-to-emerge mechanisms for supervising global markets. All of these are likely to become involved with the process of making economic adjustments in order to protect the global environment and limit the damage caused by climatic change so that the economic limitations required fall fairly and as evenly as possible across the world.

The second vital area of coordination that has to be established concerns the protection of the markets themselves from failure. While some at least of the uncontrolled and capricious consequences of the primacy of global markets may be the obvious focus of public objections, they would even more justify such complaint if their potential and sometimes actual failure were to remain untackled. The obvious and frightening possibilities of global economic collapse, which, for example, seemed to loom so large in connection with Brazil in the last months of 1998, have to be limited and controlled by global means, agreed and established by all the parties to the global economy. Market failure of one kind or another has become the most dangerous threat to the contemporary world: political and social dislocation loom, followed by a real and profound economic contraction as its consequence.

It is considerations of this kind which make it so clear why the broadest possible dissemination of the context and consequences of globalization is so important. What has to be attempted is a hard task and while natural evolution will help solutions develop, it will be equally natural for human societies to want to mould their future as much and as favourably as they can. To achieve even a measure of success will require not only a clear-eyed assessment of what is happening and why it is happening, but also a general and transnational moral assent to both the intentions and the means that are being used to bring global society to the least bad situation it can create. No one can suppose it will be easy, but it is neither unthought out nor unrealistically emotional. It is at once a limited objective and a noble ambition.

Further Reading

Agnew, John and Corbridge, Stuart, *Mastering Space: Hegemony, Territory and International Political Economy*, London, 1995

Barry Jones, R. J., *Globalization and Interdependence in the International Political Economy*, London, 1995

Biersteker, Thomas J. and Weber, Cynthia (eds), *Sovereignty as a Social Construct*, Cambridge, 1996

Brown, Seyom, *New Forces, Old Forces and the Future of World Politics: Post Cold War Edition*, New York, 1995

Buzan, Barry and Herring, Eric, *The Arms Dynamic in World Politics*, Boulder, Colo., 1998

Cerney, Philip G., *The Changing Architecture of Politics: Structure, Agency and the Future of the State*, London, 1990

Chopra, Jarat (ed.), *The Politics of Peace-Maintenance*, Boulder, Colo., 1998

Cohen, Benjamin D., *The Geography of Money*, Ithaca, 1998

Cutler, A. Claire, Haufler, Virginia and Porter, Tony (eds), *Private Authority and International Affairs*, Albany, 1999

Dicken, Peter, *Global Shift: Transforming the World Economy*, New York, 1998

Diehl, Paul F., *The Politics of Global Governance: International Organizations in an Interdependent World*, Boulder, Colo., 1996

Doremus, P., Keller, W., Pauly, L. and Reich S., *The Myth of the Global Corporation*, Princeton, 1998

Elazar, Daniel J., *Constitutionalizing Globalization: the Postmodern Revival of Confederal Arrangements*, Lanham, Md., 1998

Goddard, C. Rose, Passe-Smith, John T. and Conklin, John G. (eds), *International Political Economy: State–Market Relations in the Changing Global Order*, Boulder, Colo., 1996

Hamilton, Keith and Langhorne, Richard, *The Practice of Diplomacy: Its Evolution, Theory and Administration*, London, 1995

Held, David, *Democracy and the Global Order*, Stanford, 1995

Hewson, Martin and Sinclair, Timothy J., *Approaches to Global Governance Theory*, Albany, NY, 1999

Higgott, Richard, *Globalization*, Coventry, 1998

Hirst, P. and Thompson, G., *Globalization in Question*, London, 1996

Kaul, Inge, Grunberg, Isabelle and Stern, Marc A. (eds), *Global Public Goods: International Cooperation in the 21st Century*, OUP, New York, 1999

Keohane, Robert O. and Milner, Helen V., *Internationalization and Domestic Politics*, Cambridge, 1996

Knox, Paul and Taylor, Peter (eds), *World Cities in a World-System*, Cambridge, 1995

Martin, H. and Schumann, H., *The Global Trap: Globalization and the Assault on Property and Democracy*, London, 1997

Meier, Gerald M., *The International Environment of Business: Competition and Governance in the Global Economy*, New York, 1998

Meyer, Mary K. and Prugl, Elizabeth (eds), *Gender Politics in Global Governance*, Lanham, Md., 1998

Mittelman, James H. (ed.), *Globalization: Critical Reflections*, Boulder, Colo., 1997

Pauly, Louis, *Who Elected the Bankers: Surveillance and Control in the World Economy*, Ithaca, 1997

Piening, Christopher, *Global Europe: the European Union in World Politics*, Boulder, Colo., 1997

Rosenau, James N., *Along the Domestic–Foreign Frontier: Exploring Governance in a Turbulent World*, Cambridge, 1997

Rosenau, James N. and Czempiel, Ernst-Otto, *Governance without Government: Order and Change in World Politics*, Cambridge, 1992

Ruigrok, W. and van Tulder, R., *The Logic of International Restructuring*, London, 1995

Sassen, Saskia, *The Global City: London, New York, Tokyo*, Princeton, 1991

Sassen, Saskia, *Losing Control? Sovereignty in an Age of Globalization*, New York, 1996

Schaeffer, Robert K., *Understanding Globalization: the Social Consequences of Political, Economic and Environmental Change*, Lanham, Md., 1997

Selgson, Mitchell, A. and Passe-Smith, John T. (eds), *Development and Underdevelopment: the Political Economy of Global Inequality*, Boulder, Colo., 1998

Strange, Susan, *The Retreat of the State: the Diffusion of Power in the World Economy*, Cambridge, 1996

Strange, Susan, *Mad Money: When Markets Outgrow Governments*, Ann Arbor, 1998

Vayrynen, Raimo V. (ed.), *Globalization and Global Governance*, Lanham, Md., 1998

Vogel, Steven K., *Freer Markets, More Rules*, Ithaca, 1996

Weiss, Linda, *The Myth of the Powerless State*, Ithaca, 1998

Weiss, Thomas G. and Gordenker, Leon, *NGOs, the UN and Global Governance*, Boulder, Colo., 1996

Index